Aim to Grow Your Brain

The Secret Mindset
of Underachieving Students
&
Five Steps to Inspiring
Greater Effort

Joanne M. Billingsley, M.ED.

Foreword by Olympic Gold Medalist Josh Davis

This edition published by
Dog Ear Publishing
4010 W. 86th Street, Ste H
Indianapolis, IN 46268

www.dogearpublishing.net

ISBN: 978-160844-114-3
Library of Congress Control Number: Applied for
This book is printed on acid-free paper.

Printed in the United States of America

Dedication

To my two beautiful granddaughters, Julia Mae Williams and Eleanor Agnes Billingsley. May they be blessed with wise and dedicated teachers and develop a *growth mindset*.

TABLE OF CONTENTS

Foreword

Olympic Champion & Gold Medalist
Josh Davis

"*Thank you, Joanne, for giving us hope, the hope that – with effort, there will be progress, there will be change for the better, there will be growth*"

- Josh Davis

As a full time motivational speaker, I love reading books that inspire and bring hope. **Aim to Grow Your Brain** is one of the most inspiring books I have ever read. The information it contains shows that there is hope for the kids I work with, and for anyone else striving to learn a new skill. Every parent, teacher and student can benefit by understanding the potential for change and growth illustrated in this work. Many inspirational books are about change, but **Aim to Grow Your Brain** is truly about change you can believe in.

I have read many books, and have listened to countless motivational gurus talk about the growth mindset – in a number of ways. It has always **seemed** to me that their claims are true. **At least, I have wanted them to be true**. But, when a dedicated educator with years of classroom experience reviews the research from top scientists, and provides concrete scientific evidence, that's good stuff! After reading **Aim to Grow Your Brain**, I know without a doubt that these growth principles are true.

In remembering my preparation for the Olympics, I can look back over twenty years of training. First, I started out at ages seven to eleven playing soccer and riding my bike. From ages eleven to thirteen, I participated in every sport available to me. Finally, I spent ten years, from ages thirteen to twenty-three, on swimming.

You need to know that, for a swimmer, starting at thirteen is somewhat late; and one of my first coaches suggested I wouldn't make it as a swimmer. But another coach always gave me hope. He said, "If you do 'this' you can be pretty good...and if you do 'this and this' you could be one of the best!" And he always reminded me, over the years, that **progress follows effort.** So, no matter how hard, overwhelming and futile the journey seemed to be, I felt encouraged by that truth: **"Progress follows effort."**

During my quest for Olympic Gold, I learned that neuromuscular pathways must be constructed with repetition and focused training. Olympic athletes must put forth extreme effort over a long period to fulfill their dream and accomplish their goal. What *Aim to Grow Your Brain* clearly reveals, is that neural pathways in the brain are similar to neuromuscular pathways in the body. Focused mental effort and dedicated practice will generate new connections between neurons and expand neural networks. You can apply gold medal training to strengthen your body…and your BRAIN!

I have lived my life by several maxims that my parents, coaches, and teachers have taught me. One is that **people are equal; ideas are not**. This sounds strange and irrelevant at first, but let me explain why it is significant to me. First, people are equal. I'm not better than you – and you're not better than I am. We're just both trying to get better than we were yesterday. So – we are all on this journey of life together. Yes, life is full of milestones and markers that we make along the way, but the point is, we are all "in process."

I've learned that the greatest satisfaction in life does not really come from accumulating awards, records, money, or letters after my name. These things make a person feel more important than someone else. Although the rewards are well and good, and are to be expected and enjoyed in a lifestyle marked with effort and excellence, they tend to fade rather quickly. What really lasts is the character you build – that you are a person with a mindset of "no limits," and the will to persevere.

Never forget, that in the constant pursuit of self-improvement, enjoying the journey and helping people along the way are the things that really count. And I will say this: helping, serving, inspiring, and giving hope to others is the best way to enjoy the journey. It is true that we find our greatest joy in helping others to reach their potential. I believe that if each one of us could encourage the people in our sphere of influence to develop a "growth mindset" – that it would literally impact our whole country's future. After all, it was that mindset which made us seek freedom at the very beginning, and it has made our country prosper for nearly two and a half centuries. **The powerful message in this book is what our country desperately needs at this time.**

If someone asks me what this book is about, I will reply, "It's about hope." Kids need hope and, to be honest, teachers need hope too. Success might not come easily, but it is encouraging to know that there is hope. There is a way for kids to become more than they thought possible.

When I started swimming, I was not a prodigy. In fact, I was a novice among veterans, and a late bloomer among other individuals who performed like men at age thirteen. But I quickly learned the great equalizer of the universe...**effort.** If I worked hard enough, smart enough, and long enough, good things were going to happen. I remember a poster on my wall that said, **"If you can't win, make the one ahead of you break the record."** So I knew that if someone was going to beat me, they were going to have to be very good, and they were going to hurt badly doing it. Another poster I had said this, **"If your opponent is bigger, stronger, faster...then train harder, smarter and longer."**

To apply myself in sports was one thing, but to apply myself in school was another. I used to be afraid of reading, and used to despise writing. My mom, who is a professional pianist, did her best to encourage me in music, but I couldn't stick with it. So, even though I knew I wasn't "dumb," I went through elementary, middle, and high school convinced that I was not an intellectually gifted person – and that was that!

Then, in college, I had a breakthrough. I realized that when I applied myself, good things happened. It helped that I had a passion for it, but when I made an *A* in one of the toughest classes in the communications college, I thought: "I am smart! I can do this!"

If you had met me in high school, you would have thought I was mute; but in college, I kept taking speech classes. (God bless my teachers for suffering through my talks!) Just as with everything else in life, the more you do something the better you get at it. Now, at thirty-six, I'm the author of a book, and I'm going back to finish my college degree. Not only that – I've started piano lessons again!

My brain grew as I read this book! Your brain will grow too! You will be better equipped for one of the noblest vocations in life, helping young people to live up to their potential.

I am excited about *Aim to Grow Your Brain,* because it communicates in powerful ways the maxims I live by. They are:

- **progress follows effort**
- **people are equal, ideas are not**
- **you are a champion if you always do your best.**

The focus and drive of daily self-improvement is a tremendous reward in itself. There is no greater satisfaction in life than in doing your best every day – making yourself a better person, and creating a better world. Let this be the year that we are secure in the fact that we have done all in our power to help others, and thus to create a better world.

Thank you, Joanne, for giving us hope, the hope that – with effort, there will be progress, there will be change for the better, there will be growth.

About Josh Davis

Joshua ("Josh") Clark Davis (born September 1, 1972 in San Antonio, Texas) is a former Olympic freestyle swimmer. During his Olympic career, Josh won five medals as a member of the U.S.A. Men's Relay Teams: three gold medals at the 1996 Summer Olympic Games in Atlanta, Georgia, and two silver medals, four years later at the 2000 Summer Olympic Games in Sydney, Australia.

On February 15, 2008, Josh was inducted into the San Antonio Sports Hall of Fame. Presently, Josh is a nationally- renowned motivational speaker and master swim clinician. He resides in San Antonio, Texas with his wife Shantel and five children.

Introduction

In October of 1939, Winston Churchill used these words to describe Russia, "It is a riddle, wrapped in a mystery, inside an enigma." Churchill's quote described precisely the way I felt about Teddy. For months, I had placed before him well-crafted, engaging science lessons and activities. I had shown a personal interest in Teddy and successfully established a good relationship with him. He liked me, I liked him, and we both agreed that science was more fun than all of his other subjects. So, what was the problem? Why did Teddy remain a mystery? I'll describe my experience as Teddy's 7th grade science teacher, and let you decide.

Teddy routinely slouched in his seat, his head resting on the chair back. He was not disruptive, just disengaged most of the time. During laboratory investigations and "Learning Center" activities, when other students were buzzing around the room with excitement, Teddy's demeanor remained passive and lethargic. Frequently, he would be the last to start an assignment or activity and the first to give up when things got a little challenging. I thought he was simply one of the world's laziest kids.

Curious about his history, I made a trip to the counselor's office to pull his academic file. It was very interesting. In grades 1-5, I found mostly A's and B's. His standardized test scores painted a picture of a VERY bright student with math scores that placed him in the 99th percentile nationally. However, a quick check in the database showed that he was currently in danger of failing three of his five core 7th grade subjects. I could not blame his lack of success on lousy teachers. He was in the hands of several master teachers, and yet none of us could solve the riddle or unwrap the mystery of Teddy. He remained an enigma.

Students like Teddy kept showing up in my classroom. They scored low on the effort scale, regardless of their ability level. Like Teddy, they were the most difficult to engage and the first to quit when things got a little tough. Prodding them, verbally encouraging them, and even bribing them met with limited success.

These students said things like, "I didn't get the math gene," "My mom stinks at spelling too," or "I'm just not college material." I once asked a young man named Derek, "What do you want to do when you grow up, Derek?" and he responded, "Miss, I'll probably go to jail; my dad and all my uncles are in jail." Can you *imagine* being 12 years old and believing that you inherited the "go to jail gene" from your parents?

> For these students, effort and ability are inversely proportional. In their minds, if a task is difficult and requires considerable effort, students assume that they lack some innate (genetic) ability.

Early one morning I was sitting in traffic, slowly making my way to school while listening to NPR. The news reporter mentioned a newly published study out of Stanford University. Psychologist Carol Dweck had just released a book, titled *Mindset: The Psychology of Success*. The book suggests that students' perceptions of intelligence may profoundly influence their willingness to put forth effort, and their subsequent performance in school. Furthermore, it strongly suggests that students who are taught that intelligence is malleable – that it is not fixed or predetermined – tend to remain fully engaged, even when schoolwork is difficult for them. In short, they are more likely to persist and work hard during challenging times. This "growth mindset," as Dweck coined it, allows a student to view challenges as opportunities to *learn* and *grow*, rather than as setbacks. The message: "Smart is something you can get, not just something you are," is a transformative one for students.

Thinking about Carol Dweck's book brought up many questions. Do some students believe that "intelligence cards" are dealt at birth: some students getting the dumb cards, others the average cards, and a lucky few the smart cards? Could this be the key to understanding students like Teddy? Was it possible that his actions were motivated by misconceptions about his own intelligence? Did students like Teddy believe intelligence is cast in stone at birth? Would teaching students that they can grow their intelligence motivate them to engage in more challenging activities?

That afternoon I purchased Dweck's book *Mindset* and devoured it in a matter of hours. I had frequently encountered much of what she described during my twenty years in the classroom. I decided that Teddy needed a good neurology lesson to help him understand just how malleable human intelligence really is. He needed proof that through effort and practice he could really **GROW** his brain, sprout new dendrite connections and get smarter. In fact, all my middle school students needed to understand the implications of having an unchallenged brain. They all needed the "use it or lose it" lesson.

I knew we had students with a "fixed mindset" sitting in our classes. In fact, we had teachers with a fixed mindset teaching some of those classes. The question became, "What can I do to change this situation?"

Allowing students to slip away – seemingly past the point of no return – without trying to find a solution, is inexcusable. After years of teaching science, curriculum writing and studying middle school students, I decided it was time to explore a new strategy to reach students like Teddy.

In May 2007, I resigned my teaching job, and for the next eighteen months devoted myself to scientific research. I read every book and publication I could find on neuroplasticity. I attended neuroscience conferences and lectures, listened to countless pod casts and reviewed the work of top neuroscientists. Armed with this new information and drawing upon 20 years of classroom experience, I wrote *Aim to Grow Your Brain*.

With the first draft of the book complete, I conducted two pilot programs with middle school teachers and students. These pilot programs allowed me to witness, first hand, the impact of the message that this book delivers. Data collected during the pilots, confirmed that, **when students believe in their potential to grow a better brain** through personal effort, they try harder in challenging situations, and are more resilient.

Chapter One

"Smart is something you get, not something you are."
-J.M.B.

Why Aim to Grow Your

Brain?

Teachers refer to them as underachievers, implying such negative descriptions as slothful and unmotivated. Parents are kinder, describing them as complacent, laidback or lethargic. You find them in abundance in both middle school and high school. These students, when faced with a challenge, give up quickly. They do not embrace academic risks or rigor – and yet they complain of being bored in school. Their frustrated teachers and parents frequently proclaim, "If these kids would just try, put forth more effort, and practice faithfully, they could be successful." The question always seems to come back to this: Why do some students give their best effort when faced with a challenge, while others simply give up?

Aim to Grow Your Brain seeks an answer to this age-old question by exploring current research in the areas of neuroplasticity and psychology. The goal of this book is to equip teachers with the knowledge, skills and lessons, needed to deliver this **life-changing message of hope** to students:

> *Smart is something you get, not something you are. If you embrace new challenges, give your best effort, and practice faithfully, you will grow in intelligence. We all have the potential to grow a better brain.*
>
> *J.M.B.*

Join me, as we explore how to implement the **"five steps to inspiring greater effort and more practice."** Discover classroom-tested strategies that foster the *growth mindset*, and empower students to embrace life's challenges.

Five Steps to Inspiring Effort & Practice

1. **Analyze core beliefs about intelligence**. Discover how students' perceptions of intelligence can have a profound influence on their willingness to put forth effort, and their subsequent performance in school. Compare and contrast *growth and fixed mindsets. (Chapters 1 & 2)*

2. **Present basic lessons in neuroscience**, including brain basics, such as, the structure and function of neurons and neural networks. Learn how the brain learns. *(Chapter 3)*

3. **Review and summarize current, credible research in the area of neuroplasticity**, confirming that intelligence is malleable, and that the brain is plastic – capable of changing itself, based on life's experiences. Share inspirational, personal stories that document the effects of practice and effort. Illustrate how an enriched environment shapes the human brain. *(Chapters 4 & 5)*

4. **Evaluate current research on the effects of television, sleep, fear, and stress on the brain's structure and ability to function.** *(Chapters 6 & 7)*

5. **Teach "brain friendly" strategies** that boost student confidence while enhancing learning and improving memory. *(Chapter 8)*

Current research confirms that as long as the brain remains engaged, it will continue to shape and reshape itself. It is important for both **teachers** and **students** to know that the human brain can:

- repair damaged regions
- grow new neurons
- rezone regions that perform one task to assume a new task
- change and build new neural networks (dendrites)
- quiet or prune away networks that are seldom used

In the early 1990's, Dr. Jay Giedd of the National Institute of Mental Health began a long-term study by performing MRI's on 145 healthy patients, ages four through twenty-four. He scanned the brain of each patient every two years to look for possible anatomical changes that might occur over time. What he discovered was shocking. The MRI's revealed the adolescent brain was undergoing significant restructuring and responding rapidly to environmental influences. The research suggests that an enriched and challenging environment can play a powerful role in shaping the teenage brain. If teens read frequently, they will quickly become better readers; if they practice challenging math problems, those networks grow, and students will become efficient problem-solvers. The conclusion…there is an excellent opportunity during adolescence to build a better brain (Giedd 1999).

Science has revealed that most of the changes that take place in the brain are a result of what we do and what we experience. In a sense, the lives we live and the decisions we make determine the brain's structure: the size of its different regions, the strength of connections between one area and another, and the speed at which impulses travel. It is true that we are each born with a unique brain because of genetic inheritance, but it is equally true that we spend a lifetime sculpting and shaping the brain as we live out our lives. What a gift, to be able to grow and sculpt your brain! What a responsibility!

Step 1

Discover the Secret Mindset

Of Underachieving Students

Analyze core beliefs about intelligence. Discover how students' perceptions of intelligence can have a profound influence on their willingness to put forth effort, and their subsequent performance in school. Explore and compare the *growth and fixed mindsets*.

Chapter Two

"The growth mindset lets people – even those who are targets of negative labels – use and develop their minds fully. Their heads are not filled with limiting thoughts, a fragile sense of belonging, and a belief that other people can define them."
- Dr. Carol Dweck

Two Mindsets

Learners and Nonlearners

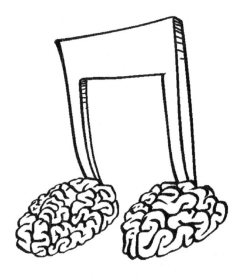

Benjamin Barber, a well-known sociologist, once said, "I don't divide the world into the weak and the strong, or the successful and the failures ... I divide the world into the learners and the nonlearners." The question arises: Why are some people learners and others nonlearners? Could it be that some are born smart – with a natural desire to learn, while others enter this world lacking ability and the ambition to acquire knowledge?

Dr. Carol Dweck, a leading researcher in the field of developmental psychology, has conducted some interesting research to explore these very questions. In her research, she concludes that one's core beliefs about intelligence can have a profound impact on their attitude toward learning. Dweck identified two different mindsets or "belief systems" that appear to unfold in childhood and stay with us throughout adulthood. In her study (with 7th grade students), she documents that the *fixed* and *growth* mindsets can have a powerful influence on a student's willingness to put forth effort, and their subsequent performance in school.

What are the characteristics of the two contrasting mindsets? Carol Dweck contends that individuals who are perceived as learners likely have a "growth mindset." This growth mindset is based on the belief that basic qualities (intelligence, character, personality) are things we can cultivate, change and grow through effort and practice. Individuals with the growth mindset look at difficult challenges as an opportunity to get smarter, a chance to learn something new. They do not want to waste time proving how great they are; they are more interested in getting better. When someone with a growth mindset experiences failure, that person sees it as a temporary setback or an opportunity to grow and learn. Individuals with a growth mindset believe that more effort results in more ability.

In contrast, the nonlearners appear to have a "fixed mindset." A fixed mindset is based on the belief that basic qualities are set in stone and are mostly unchangeable. This group believes that intelligence, character, athletic abilities, etc. are predetermined by genetics, that they are inherited. An individual with the fixed mindset is overly concerned about hiding deficiencies, believing that they are permanent. These individuals feel a need to prove that they are smart or to hide the fact they are not smart. They will not take risks, and they avoid challenging situations for fear of failure.

We can all agree that babies and young children are born with a healthy amount of ambition. No matter how many times little ones stumble or falter in their initial efforts to walk and talk, they keep on trying, determined to master their amazing new skills. Young children see a positive relationship between effort and ability. They hold the belief that ability is gained through effort; that is, if you try hard and put forth effort, you will succeed. Their attitude is, "I just need to keep trying. If I do, I will eventually figure it out."

By the age of 11 or 12, however, children's views of ability and effort often begin to change. Suddenly, many middle school students begin to believe that effort and ability vary inversely (Nicholls 1990). For them, more effort implies less ability; that is, if you try hard and fail, you must lack some natural ability. As children move from elementary into middle school, many begin to lose their natural drive to learn, become discouraged, and end up joining the ranks of underachievers.

If you are not convinced that this shift in mindset occurs, try this: ask a class of kindergarteners how many artists are in the room and watch what happens. Nearly every hand in the room shoots into the air. Ask the same question to a group of middle school students, and you might have two or three students raise their hands. Finally, try asking the question again at your next faculty meeting. What you may discover, is that not even the art teacher will raise his or her hand.

Why would an art teacher not claim to be an artist? The answer is that such a teacher has the fixed mindset perspective. The teacher thinks: "The fact that I have earned a college degree in art does not make me an artist. Artistic ability is a gift, bestowed at birth. A person can learn to teach art, but they can not learn to be an artist."

The belief that characteristics such as artistic giftedness and intelligence are fixed at an early age runs deep. Year after year, middle school students say such things as, "Sorry, Ms. B., I stink at math and science, I guess I just didn't get the math and science gene from my parents."

Having been a middle school teacher for nearly twenty years, I have concluded that most middle school students identify themselves as belonging to one of three groups: the smart group, the average group or the not-so-smart group. While many recognize that they can learn new things in school, they do not expect or believe in their ability to change groups. They believe that genetics has dealt them a set of intelligence cards, and they hold them firmly, fearful of revealing their hand.

One elementary school teacher had this to say, "Once assigned to the Bluebird Reading Group, students develop the "bluebird mindset" and there they expect to stay, with little expectation of receiving a promotion or a demotion." Intelligence, they believe, is cast in stone.

Shifting Students to a Growth Mindset

If having a growth mindset is an important key to success in school, why can't we simply tell our students that intelligence is malleable and then sit back and watch them flourish? Before you look for an answer, keep in mind that the two most frequently asked questions in a middle school classroom are, "Why do we have to learn this?" followed by "How do you know this is true?"

I remember trying to convince my seventh grade science students that all objects, regardless of their mass, fall to the earth at the same rate. I had two tennis balls, one regular tennis ball and one I had cut a slit in and stuffed with pennies. The kids placed bets on which tennis ball would hit the ground first when dropped from a balcony. Despite the illustration in their science book, and my insistence that the tennis balls would hit the ground at the same time, they placed bets heavily in favor of the "penny ball" landing first.

With the gravity experiment permanently etched in memory, I realized that middle school kids would demand scientific evidence that the brain can indeed grow in intelligence. Ironically, I soon discovered that students would not be the only ones to demand proof that intelligence is changeable. Many teachers and parents are firmly entrenched in the fixed mindset, and they need evidence as well. I once overheard a teacher say, "I don't know what they expect me to do. Some kids were obviously behind the door when the brains were passed out. Do they expect me to perform a miracle?" If only that teacher understood the miraculous nature of the human brain!

Providing Evidence & Inspiring Effort

Much has been written about the brain and learning over the past ten years. In 2006, Pierce Howard released the third edition to *The Owner's Manual for the Brain,* and it was over 1000 pages long! Educators are anxious to utilize recent discoveries about the brain in their teaching, and neuroscientists and educators have come together to share their secrets. However, even with all of this new collaboration, many teachers feel overwhelmed with the complexity of the scientific research and, surprisingly, almost all students have been left completely out of the information loop.

In 1913, the great Spanish neuroscientist, Ramon y Cajal, was quoted as saying, "In the adult centers the nerve paths are something fixed, ended and immutable" but he continued, "It is for the science of the future to change, if possible, this harsh decree." Many of the stories that follow in this book, will reveal, that science has done precisely that.

The lessons (found at the end of chapter two), will allow students an opportunity to reflect on how their core beliefs about intelligence can influence behavior. Share and discuss the lesson with your students, and together you can experience and appreciate the power of the growth mindset!

Dawdlers & Daydreamers

Look over your current class roster. How many of your students fit the Emily mold? (Take a minute and read Lesson 2.2) How many abandon challenging tasks and dawdle, daydream, or begin an easier activity? As a classroom teacher, I routinely found many of my students to be like Emily – resistant to academic challenges.

If given a list of activity options for a class project, they pick the easiest activity, even over one that they find more interesting. Some might say that choosing the easier assignment particularly for a middle school student, is simply human nature, to be expected and not alarming. But as Dweck states in her book, *Mindset,* "It's one thing to pass up a puzzle. It's another to pass up an opportunity that's important to your future." What could account for Emily's lack of enthusiasm for puzzle solving? Could it be the fixed mindset, fear of not looking smart, and fear of failure?

In many high schools, enrollment in advanced math and science classes continues to drop, despite efforts to encourage students to sign up. Teachers are told to increase the challenge, but students and parents complain when assignments are too difficult. What might inspire students to embrace a more rigorous curriculum and register for that Chemistry II class? Perhaps, sharing some real life stories, depicting the fixed and growth mindset could give them a new perspective. Let's begin our examination of the fixed and growth mindsets with tales of two world-class athletes.

John McEnroe and Michael Jordan were immensely talented athletes. McEnroe occupied the number one spot on the men's tennis circuit for many years, while Jordan won every award that professional basketball had to offer. Both men had very successful athletic careers. Yet, when you read their respective biographies, you can detect a sharp contrast between the two men. One man was a classic example of the "fixed mindset," the other personified the "growth mindset."

Carefully read the two biographies that follow (Lessons 2.3 & 2.4). Think about the characteristics associated with the fixed and growth mindsets. Read and discuss the two biographies with your students. Have them write a story about someone they know who exemplifies the growth mindset. Ask them which athlete they most identify with and why.

Lesson 2.1

A Baby's Mindset

Do you realize that you had mastered two of the most difficult tasks of your lifetime before your third birthday? The first was a very difficult physical challenge and chances are you had accomplished it by the time you turned one year old. Any guesses? If you said, "learning to walk," you were absolutely right.

The next major obstacle to conquer was an intellectual skill. This one took you a little longer to master, but like most kids, you were well on your way to becoming proficient by 36 months. The challenging intellectual skill I am referring to. You guessed it - learning to talk. The average eighteen-month-old child has a vocabulary of 600-1200 words. Few people remember what it was like to face and conquer these two tasks, so let's refresh your memory.

Watching a baby learn to walk is both intriguing and comical. First, babies learn to roll over. They flop from their backs to their tummies and from their tummies to their backs, often learning to roll all the way across a room.

Next, they focus on "getting up on all fours". They spend most of their waking hours practicing, rocking back and forth until they finally lurch forward. The result: forward progress, rug burns on the knees and nose, and the ultimate reward, crawling. Many parents report that babies are consumed with practicing while they are learning to crawl. Babies might experience disrupted sleeping patterns or lose interest in eating while they are learning this new skill.

Next comes the pulling up stage. Now that they are crawling, they can get to that coffee table, reach up, and pull themselves to a standing position. Slowly but surely, they learn to let go with their little hands and stand alone, unsupported and free. This requires an almost constant adjustment in balance, something you now do naturally without thought. At this stage, babies experience failure repeatedly. Two unsteady steps and plop, down they go. Their resilience is remarkable.

After weeks of diligent practice, one foot is placed in front of the other and all those little steps turn into walking. It is amazing how quickly babies progress, from taking three unsteady steps, to streaking so fast their parents must run to catch them. Yes, they fall down frequently when they are learning. Yes, they get bumps, bruises, and scratches on their knees. But have you ever known of a baby who decided learning to walk was too hard, and who gave up trying because it was too difficult? Babies seem immune to their failures; all of that falling down, all of those failed attempts simply mean they need to keep practicing. They keep trying and practicing until walking and talking become effortless. Failure is not a word in their vocabulary… yet.

Student Reflection Questions:

1. Do you think this "baby mindset" changes, as the baby gets older? If yes, explain how and why it might change.

2. What would it be like if the "baby mindset" stayed with us into adulthood?

Lesson 2.2

Students are Sometimes Puzzling

Emily and Nathan each get a series of puzzles from their teacher. The first puzzle is easy, but each new one becomes more difficult.

Emily: *I finished the first three! These others aren't much fun. They're too hard.*

Nathan doesn't answer for a while. He is busy trying to solve a difficult puzzle.

Nathan: *Got it! Boy! Some of these puzzles are tough!*

Nathan continues the puzzles while Emily sits quietly for a while, and then takes out paper and decides to draw – an activity she likes.

Nathan: *Don't you want to do the other puzzles? They're pretty cool, they just take a little longer to figure out.*

Emily: *Those are boring. They're too hard. I don't want to waste my time.*

After a while, Nathan finds a puzzle he can't solve, so he goes up to the teacher.

Nathan: *Is it OK if I take this puzzle home to solve? I think with a little more time I can solve it. I don't know why, but I love these things (puzzles) even if they are hard to solve. The harder they are to solve, the more I like them!*

Student Reflection Questions:

1. Why do you think Emily is so easily discouraged when the puzzles get more difficult?

2. Why might some students be fearful of academic challenges and others willing to try them, even if they risk failure?

Lesson 2.3

John McEnroe - Bad Boy of Tennis

Pow! The two-year-old hit a tennis ball with his little racquet.

Yeaaa! The crowd erupted in cheers; the crowd being mom, dad, grandparents, and friends – a captive audience.

Whack! Another roar from the crowd!

"This is fun," thought the boy, John McEnroe. "Just look at all the attention I'm getting. I get more notice hitting the tennis ball than when I try to be cute, or even when I throw a tantrum. I'm just going to figure out how to hit the ball every time."

As John grew, he excelled at tennis. He won several junior tennis tournaments, but he was never first on the junior circuit. Not being number one was difficult for McEnroe to accept. For him, tennis was about rankings and proving to the world that he was the best.

As a teenager, McEnroe attended Trinity School in Manhattan, an Ivy League preparatory school. It was during this time that John's temptation to be a "class clown" got him into trouble. He played a prank that caused him to be suspended from the Port Washington Tennis Academy for six months. As a result, his parents moved him to the Cove Racquet Club, where he worked with the famous pro trainer, Palafox.

After high school, many exciting opportunities came John's way. He was able to play in Europe, where he won the French Juniors Tournament. Then he aimed for the junior's title at Wimbledon, but he wound up qualifying for the men's competition instead. There, he advanced to the semi-finals, where the more experienced Jimmy Connors beat him. McEnroe was, nevertheless, quite the young prodigy, the youngest man to reach the semi-finals of Wimbledon.

At this point, the enthusiasm for tennis he had experienced as a child had started to fade. McEnroe was losing the ability to accept setbacks as learning experiences. He was out to prove his worth, and failure was like a personal affront. Letting his temper get the upper hand, he reacted in a manner that many considered unsportsmanlike and was labeled one of the "bad boys of tennis."

Newsweek magazine's Pete Axthelm deplored McEnroe's actions by writing, "He is a young man who raised perfectly placed strokes to a high art form, only to resort to tantrums that smear his masterpieces like graffiti." However, even after the criticism, and after inconsistent winnings for the rest of the year, McEnroe became *Tennis* magazine's *Rookie of the Year* for 1977.

After being named *Rookie of the Year*, McEnroe received a tennis scholarship to Stanford University in Palo Alto, California, and led his team to the NCAA Championship in 1978. The following year, he decided to leave school and turn pro. During his first half-year as a pro, he made nearly half a million dollars. Very impressive!

Unfortunately, as McEnroe gained fame, his setbacks caused more outbursts. George Plimpton defended McEnroe's antics in *Esquire* magazine: "He's the only player in the history of the game to go berserk and play better tennis."

Between 1981 and 1984, McEnroe was at the peak of his professional career. He won a total of seven Grand Slam titles in singles, and seven Grand Slam titles in doubles. The ATP rated him number one in its year-end ranking from 1981 to 1984.

In 1985, McEnroe's success began to decline. He won eight singles tournaments that year, but no Grand Slam events. Some people blamed his declining performance on a lack of systematic training. Another factor that worked against him, though, was his lack of self-control. In a fit of anger, he bounced his racket and began yelling obscenities at the 1990 Australian Open – behavior that earned a default. Sally Jenkins of *Sports Illustrated* made this sad observation: "McEnroe's seven Grand Slam titles amount to about half of what he could have won had he bothered to train properly and gain control of his temper."

John McEnroe once said, "Some people don't want to rehearse; they just want to perform. Other people want to practice a hundred times first; I'm in the first group." McEnroe did not take pride in effort and practice. He relied on his "natural giftedness." When he lost, he blamed others; he made excuses. One time the weather was too hot, the next too cold. He lost because he had a fever, a headache, a backache, because he ate too much or too little before the match. He lost because a cameraman distracted him or because the line judge cheated him out of a point. The list of excuses was long and varied.

Failure did not motivate John McEnroe, it demoralized him and caused him to doubt his ability. In 1979, he played mixed doubles at Wimbledon. During the match, John lost his serve three times and he and his partner lost in three straight sets. For McEnroe, that was the ultimate embarrassment. He was quoted as saying, "That's it. I'm never playing doubles again. I can't handle this." It was twenty years before he stepped onto the court to play mixed doubles again. John McEnroe did not embrace opportunities to grow and improve. Instead, he avoided failure.

Student Reflection:

1. Write a descriptive paragraph about someone you know that reflects the *fixed mindset*. What behaviors do they demonstrate that suggests a *fixed mindset*?

Lesson 2.4

Michael Jordan - His "Airness"

Michael Jeffrey Jordan was born in Brooklyn, New York on February 17, 1963. He was the fourth of five children. His father, James, was a mechanic, and his mother, Deloris, worked as a bank teller. Shortly after Michael was born, the family moved to Wilmington, North Carolina. Like many young boys, Michael played Little League baseball and football. But, ultimately, it was his skill on the basketball court that made Michael Jordan legendary.

His fans called him "His Airness," "Air Jordan" or "MJ." During Jordan's record performance of 63 points in the playoffs against the Boston Celtics, Larry Bird, also a talented basketball player, claimed that Jordan was "God disguised as Michael Jordan." ESPN voted Jordan "The greatest athlete of the twentieth century."

Because of Jordan's countless shots and high-flying moves to win games, basketball enthusiasts consider him the world's greatest clutch player. Few who saw the game will ever forget when Michael Jordan won his sixth and last NBA championship – with a steal and a shot in the closing seconds.

It is hard to believe that in his sophomore year of high school, Jordan was cut from the basketball team. The coach at Laney High School concluded that Michael, at 5'11", was too small for the team, and that his talent was too raw. For Jordan, being cut from the team presented a challenge – one that he would face with determination.

The summer after being cut from the team, he worked tirelessly, spending countless hours practicing and perfecting his game. The following year, as a junior, Jordan made the team and averaged 25 points per game. Then, as a senior, he had the honor of being named to the McDonald's All-American Team.

Michael experienced the excitement and reward of overcoming a difficult challenge. He understood the value of effort and practice, and once said, "Obstacles don't have to stop you. If you run into a wall, don't turn around and give up. Figure out a way to climb it, go through it, or work around it." His philosophy: "I can accept failure, but I can't accept not trying." Clearly, with this mindset, he was destined to succeed.

Following high school, Jordan accepted a scholarship from North Carolina University. In 1982, he led the Tarheels to the NCAA Championship. The championship game concluded with Michael taking and making the game-winning shot. It was a challenge that he accepted repeatedly throughout his professional career.

Once asked about the pressure of taking the last shot, Jordan replied, "I've missed more than 9,000 shots in my career. I've lost almost 300 games. Twenty-six times, I've been trusted to take the game winning shot and missed. I've failed over and over and over again in my life. And that is why I succeed." This was the mindset of the man known as the greatest clutch basketball player in the history of the game.

In the 1984 NBA draft, the Chicago Bulls selected Jordan with the third overall pick. Although he left college a year early, Jordan returned to the university in 1986 to complete his degree in geography. No challenge left unfinished!

His early years as a pro were successful, but Michael continually saw opportunities for improvement. His three-point shooting average was a disappointing 14% his rookie year, but by the time he retired from the game it was 40%. Known for his poor defense as a rookie, he soon became a regular on the NBA All-Defensive team. Despite achieving fame and fortune, Michael Jordan never stopped searching for ways to improve his game.

Michael Jordan had a career filled with awards and accolades. He would go on to win five regular season MVP awards, six NBA championships, three All-Star game MVP awards, and two Olympic Gold Medals. Jordan was a ferocious competitor on the basketball court. But for him, the game was about more than just winning. It was about pushing himself to new limits, and finding new ways to grow. "I've always believed that if you put in the work, the results will come," Jordan said. "You have to expect things of yourself before you can do them."

Examining Core Beliefs about Intelligence

The John McEnroe and Michael Jordan biographies illustrate two very different mindsets. Test your ability to distinguish between the two mindsets by completing the Mindset Questionnaire, found on the next page. Can you identify which statements personify the *fixed mindset* and which reflect the *growth mindset*?

After discussing the two mindsets and sharing the biographies of John McEnroe and Michael Jordan with your students, provide them with a copy of the questionnaire. Encourage them to analyze the 25 statements and see if they can distinguish between those statements that reflect the *fixed mindset*, and those statements that reflect the *growth mindset*. Ask them to reflect in writing on their core beliefs about intelligence.

Student Reflection:

1. Write an informative essay, comparing and contrasting the *fixed* and *growth* mindsets.

Mindset Questionnaire

Read each statement carefully. Place an **F** in front of the statement if you think the statement reflects the *"fixed mindset"*; place a **G** in front of the statement if you think the statement reflects the *"growth mindset."*

1. Human qualities, such as intellectual skills, can grow through effort.

2. Smart people generally make few mistakes.

3. If you struggle in school and fail, it is probably because you are not very smart.

4. You inherit your intelligence from your parents. If your parents are smart you will probably be smart too.

5. Smart people usually do not experience failure.

6. Regardless of how much sports ability you have (or don't have); you can always change or improve it quite a bit.

7. If you find school difficult, it is probably because you are not very smart.

8. You can grow your intelligence if you try hard and put forth a lot of effort.

9. Human qualities such as intellectual skills are inherited and are mostly unchangeable.

10. You can learn new information, but you cannot change your IQ or intelligence.

11. Smart people avoid failure at all costs.

12. If you have to try really hard in school to get good grades, it is probably because you are not very smart.

13. You can always change basic things about the kind of person you are.

14. Smart kids don't have to try very hard in school.

15. Intelligence is fixed or genetic, you can't really change it.

16. Your brain is always changing.

17. When your body stops growing and maturing, your brain also reaches maturity and stops growing.

18. Your brain changes and can grow throughout your lifetime.

19. By the time a students reaches 4th grade you can usually tell how smart they will be.

20. Your intelligence is something very basic about you that you can't really change.

21. No matter how much effort you expend, you can not fundamentally change your intelligence

22. Your sports ability is something very basic about you and you just can't change it very much.

23. Smart kids are born smart; not-so-smart kids are born not-so-smart.

24. You can do things differently, but the important parts of who you are can't really be changed.

25. You can grow (increase) your intelligence.

Tips for Implementing Lessons

Chapter Two

Lesson 2.1 - A Baby's Mindset

Main Idea: We all start out life with a "can do" attitude – embracing and mastering difficult physical and mental challenges. A baby's determination, when learning to walk and talk, exemplifies the *growth mindset.*

Suggestions:
- Read the lesson with your students, and discuss the reflection questions.
- Encourage students to share one of their baby pictures and to write a funny story about something that happened when they were a baby.

Lesson 2.2 - Students are Sometimes Puzzling

Main Idea: As children get older, some begin to lose the baby's mindset *(growth mindset)*, and shift toward a *fixed mindset*. Nathan is excited when faced with challenging puzzles, while Emily is easily discouraged, and quickly exclaims that the puzzles are boring. The dialogue between Nathan and Emily reveals that a person's mindset affects his or her behavior and willingness to put forth effort in difficult situations.

Suggestions:
- Read the lesson with your students, and discuss the reflection questions.
- Read the following quote to your students and ask them to explain and elaborate on it.

"It's one thing to pass up a puzzle. It's another to pass up an opportunity that's important to your future."
Carol Dweck

Lesson 2.3 - John McEnroe

Main Idea: John McEnroe's biography exemplifies the *fixed mindset.* His decisions and actions are rigid and inflexible; they lack the pliability that indicates growth.

Suggestions:
- After reading the McEnroe biography, assist students in compiling a list of characteristics that describe the fixed mindset.
- Read the description of the fixed mindset below. Ask students to highlight evidence in the McEnroe biography that suggests he has a fixed mindset.

The *fixed mindset* is the belief that basic human qualities are set in stone and are unchangeable. People with a fixed mindset believe that intelligence and character – as well as athletic, artistic and musical talents – are mostly determined by genetics; that they are inherited. An individual with a fixed mindset is concerned about hiding deficiencies, and will not take risks, avoiding challenging situations for fear of failure. He or she believes that if something requires a lot of effort, the difficulty must be due to a lack some innate ability.

- Encourage students to provide examples of other individuals who exemplify the fixed mindset.

Lesson 2.4 - Michael Jeffery Jordan

Main Idea: Michael Jordan's biography exemplifies the *growth mindset*. His growth mindset is reflected in his decisions and actions.

Suggestions:

- After reading the Jordan biography, assist students in compiling a list of characteristics that describe the growth mindset.

- Read the description of the growth mindset below. Ask students to highlight evidence in the Jordan biography that suggests he has a growth mindset.

The **growth mindset** is the belief that intelligence, character, and other abilities can improve through effort and practice. Individuals with the growth mindset look at difficult challenges as opportunities to get smarter, or to learn something new. When someone with a growth mindset experiences failure, that person sees it as a **temporary** setback, or an opportunity to grow and learn. Individuals with the growth mindset believe that more effort results in more ability.

- Encourage students to provide examples of other individuals who exemplify the growth mindset.

Lesson 2.5 - Mindset Questionnaire

Main Idea: The questionnaire will help students review the characteristics of the fixed and growth mindsets.

Suggestions:

- Provide an opportunity for students to reflect and answer in writing the following question: Would you describe yourself as having a *fixed,* or a *growth* mindset? Explain, and give four examples to support your answer.

Step 2

Review brain basics. Discover how the brain learns and expands neural networks.

Present basic lessons in neuroscience, including brain basics, such as, the structure and function of neurons and neural networks.

Chapter Three

"If you look at the anatomy, the structure, the function, there's nothing in the universe that's more beautiful, that's more complex, than the human brain."
- Keith Black

Reviewing Brain Basics

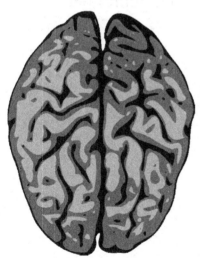

It is about the size of a cantaloupe, but has the texture of a ripe avocado. Like a walnut, it has two wrinkled halves, encased in a hard shell. It floats in a space between your ears that is large enough to hold about four cans of soda. While you are awake, it generates about 25 watts of power – enough to illuminate a light bulb. Even though it accounts for only 2% of total body mass, it consumes 20% of the body's energy. It is the most complex organ ever discovered. Now we know that when you exercise and challenge it, the brain will grow in speed and accuracy.

The average adult human brain weighs about 3 pounds. It is the most complex organ in the body, controlling virtually all human activity. It regulates heart rate, breathing, digestion, and many other unconscious activities. The brain also receives and processes information, stores memories, regulates emotions, generates thoughts and actions, and gives us our unique personalities.

The brain is divided into regions, and up until recently, scientists have thought that each region has one specific function. However, after decades of the "one location, one function" theory, scientists have discovered that the brain has the ability to rezone regions that were thought to perform specific tasks, and have them assume new tasks. In one dramatic experiment, young ferrets learned to see using the auditory region rather than the visual cortex (Sur 2000). The different regions of the brain are connected to one another by large bundles of neurons allowing allow them to communicate and coordinate their activities.

Basic regions of the brain include the cerebrum, the brainstem, and the cerebellum (see figure 1).

- The **cerebrum** is the largest region in the human brain. It is divided into the right and left hemispheres, which in turn are connected by the corpus callosum. The cerebrum is responsible for speaking, sensing, remembering, planning, reasoning, decision-making, learning, and thinking. Often referred to as "the CEO center," the cerebrum is the area of the brain that makes us uniquely human.

- The **brainstem** connects the brain with the spinal cord, and is responsible for automatic functions of the body, including heartbeat, eye movement, swallowing, breathing and sneezing.

- The **cerebellum** is at the top of the brainstem and behind the cerebrum. Scientists once thought it controlled only balance and movement, but recent research suggests that it is also involved in remembering well-learned and rehearsed tasks, skilled movement, and the coordination of thoughts.

- The **limbic system**, buried deep within the cerebrum, is sometimes referred to as the midbrain. This region regulates body temperature, thirst and appetite. It also processes memories for long-term storage, and allows us to feel pleasure. The **amygdala**, a specialized structure within the limbic system, processes emotions related to survival, such as fear and anger.

Complex circuits of neurons must work together to ensure smooth coordination between the different regions of the brain. This network of neurons, with more than 100 trillion connections, is the most complicated arrangement of matter in the known universe. It is no wonder they say, "A mind is a terrible thing to waste!"

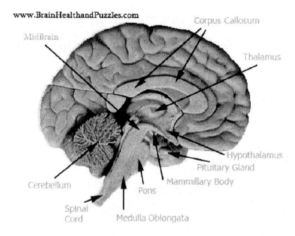

Figure 1: Basic Regions of the Human Brain

If you have never seen, touched, or explored a real brain, I strongly suggest completing the sheep brain lab (Lesson 3.1) with your students. You need 4-5 specimens per 30 students, and you can use these specimens over several class periods. Virtual dissections are available on the web, but in my opinion, they are a poor substitute for the real thing. If you are uncomfortable with doing the activity alone, ask a science teacher on the faculty to assist you. Exploring the structures of a mammalian brain is an experience your students will never forget!

Looking at the Inside of the Brain

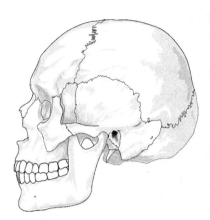

We can only guess when man first looked at the interior of the human skull. Maybe a terrible hunting accident or traumatic battle injury first exposed the brain for observation. From archaeological evidence, we know that between 10,000 – 5,000 B.C., prehistoric man intentionally cut or drilled open human skulls, and that the patients survived. By the New Stone Age (3,000-2,000 B.C.), trephination (brain surgery of the skull) was widely practiced in Western Europe, South America, and Asia.

Early civilizations believed that evil spirits could live in the head. A hole, drilled in the skull, allowed the evil spirits to escape. Trephination was likely carried out to treat epilepsy, mental illness, or severe headaches. Some tribal leaders might even have several holes drilled in their skull, so that evil spirits could continuously escape. Lucky tribal leaders!

Of the 10,000 well-preserved pre-Inca mummies discovered in Peru, more than 500 showed evidence of trephination. Some of the mummies had undergone trephination on several occasions, having multiple holes all over the skull. It has been estimated that at least 50% of the patients undergoing trephination survived the procedure. These early neurosurgeons were some of the first to observe the human brain.

Modern neurosurgeons are still probing, scanning, and studying the human brain. Fortunately, advances in technology have eliminated the need for trephination. Today, fMRI's (Functional Magnetic Resonance Images) allow scientists to observe the brain as it processes information, reacts, and reasons. It does not, however, require an expensive fMRI to view the basic components that allow the brain to function with such speed and grace. Unbelievably, a simple microscope and a prepared slide of human brain tissue (available from any biological supply company) are the only things needed.

Neural Networks Are Knowledge

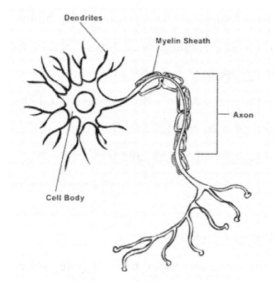

Let's begin our exploration of the inside of the brain by examining a slice of brain tissue under the microscope. Zoom in on a small slice of brain tissue and you see a dense, tangled, network of cells. These nerve cells, responsible for brain activity, are *neurons* and the billions of connections between them form our *neural network*. Neurons are the building blocks of the brain. To the naked eye, neurons look gray in color, hence the term "gray matter" is used when describing our brain tissue. Amazingly, it is these neural networks that store, produce, and share all of our knowledge.

To understand the fundamentals of how the brain learns and grows, we need to review a few basic details about the structure and function of neurons. Fortunately, we do not need to delve into the complexities of neuroscience to gain some insight into how brain plasticity (change) takes place.

Most neurons or nerve cells have five fundamental parts: **the cell body, the dendrites, the axon, the myelin sheath, and the axon terminal.** The central portion (or head) of the neuron is the *cell body*, which contains a spherical nucleus that functions like a switchboard.

The cell body has *dendrites* branching out from it. Dendrites branch out to receive in-coming chemical messages from the axon terminals of surrounding neurons. The dendrites then generate electrical signals that travel toward the cell body, which transmits these electrical impulses to its long, tail-like structure – the *axon*.

The axons of many types of neurons are surrounded by a fatty, segmented covering called the *myelin sheath*. This covering acts as a kind of insulation, enhancing the speed and ability of the axon to carry nerve impulses. At the end of the tail-like axon, you find collection of branching fibers called the ***axon terminal***. Special chemicals called neurotransmitters, important for neuron communication are located in the axon terminal.

The space where the axon terminal of one neuron establishes a connection with the dendrites of a neighboring neuron is the synaptic gap. Neurotransmitters float across this gap. In other words, the neurotransmitters leave the axon terminal of one neuron, and float over to the dendrites of another neuron – all at lightning speed. This is how neurons communicate with one another.

Dr. Gabrielle de Courten-Myers, a professor of neuropathology at the University of Cincinnati, studied brain slices from 11 cadavers and estimated that the human brain has about 23 billion neurons. Other scientists have suggested that the average adult brain may have as many as 100 billion neurons. It is important to understand, however, that it is **not the number of neurons** that determines intelligence; rather it is **how they are connected!** A single neuron, because of its many branching dendrites, can have up to 10,000 connections. Amazingly, the number and strength of these neural connections increases when the brain is exercised and challenged.

The hardware and circuits of the brain are not fixed at birth, as was once thought, but are more plastic and malleable than we ever imagined. We now know that through effort and practice, the brain will grow and expand its neural networks.

Learning, it turns out, creates a **physical change** in the brain. It occurs as new and stronger connections are made within neural networks.There is a neural network in our brain for everything we know. **Learning really is about making more connections!**

When I see students focused and working hard on a task, I like to envision what is happening inside their brains. I picture dendrites growing, expanding their network, and making new connections. I can visualize the neural web of knowledge growing more sophisticated and complex with each new discovery and association.

More importantly, though, I want my students to visualize this process as well. I want them to become aware of how their actions and choices affect their brain structure. Most students are amazed and excited to learn that they have the power to expand their neural networks. They are equally shocked to discover that when the brain is bored and unchallenged, neural networks shrink, and gray matter disappears. The thought of the brain shrinking, of actually losing intelligence, is a sobering one, for both teachers and students.

Demonstrating the Parts of a Neuron

Remember, understanding neuron structure is fundamental to understanding how the brain learns and grows. To help students understand how neurons work, try the following activity:

First, ask students to place one of their hands at the top of a blank sheet of paper, and to trace around their fingers and palm – continuing about five inches past the wrist. Next, ask students to add three labels to the drawing:

- Label the five fingers – dendrites.
- Label the palm – cell body.
- Label the arm – axon.

Finally, ask students to add arrows to their drawings, demonstrating how impulses travel as they pass from neuron to neuron. Remember, electrical impulses begin in the dendrites, progress towards the cell body, and finally travel down the axon, where the messages are transmitted to a neighboring neuron.

After students have completed their drawings, check their understanding by asking them to follow these directions:

1. Please stretch out your dendrites and wiggle them back and forth. (Students should extend their fingers and wiggle them about.)
2. Press your two cell bodies together. (Students should press the palms of their hands together.)
3. Now extend your axons towards the ceiling. (Students should extend their hands up over their heads.)

4. Pull your cell bodies apart until your axons are parallel to the floor. (Students' arms should be stretched out to the sides forming a letter "T".)

5. Now, do ten jumping jacks. Did you know that physical exercise is good for the brain?

6. Finally, ask each student to tape his or her neuron picture (hand model) to the classroom wall, aligning the pictures so that the axon of one neuron would connect to the dendrites (fingers) of the adjacent neuron, making a long strand of neurons that could communicate.

Review the student lessons and activities that follow at the end of this chapter. These lessons and activities will greatly enhance your students' understanding of neuron structure and its relationship to learning. Making neuron models from clay is a student favorite. It was fascinating to discover, that after providing 150 different students with materials and instructions on how to create a neuron model, no two of the 150 models created were exactly alike. Each model, like each student's neural network, was unique!

Lesson 3.1

Sheep Brain Lab

During the sheep brain lab, your group will function as a team of neurosurgeons. You will observe and study the sheep brain to learn more about your own human brain.

Sheep brains, although much smaller than human brains, have similar features and structures. During this observation, you will see for yourself what the cerebrum, cerebellum, spinal cord, gray and white matter, and other parts of the brain look like!

It is extremely important to treat the preserved specimen (sheep brain) with respect. These sheep brains were acquired from animals raised for their meat. No animals were sacrificed solely for the purpose of this observation.

As you read and follow directions, you will come across questions. At the end of each question is a number in parenthesis (1). Stop and find the matching number on the **Student Observation Report,** and answer the question before you continue your observations.

At the conclusion of this activity, your team will place ten **flag pins** in the brain specimen. Each pin will mark the location of a specific brain structure.

Part 1: Read and Follow Steps 1-7

Observations: External (outside) Top View

1. You will need a preserved sheep brain for the dissection and observations. Set the brain down so that the flatter side rests on the dissection pan. Note that the brain has two obvious halves, or **hemispheres**. A deep groove separates the right and left hemispheres.

2. Carefully observe the surface and shape of the **cerebrum** and the **cerebellum**. The cerebrum is the part of the brain associated with rational thought. The cerebellum is involved in the coordination of movements, thoughts and balance. How are these two regions of the brain (cerebrum and cerebellum) different from one another? (1)

3. Look at the surface of the cerebrum and locate the ridges (called **gyri**) and the grooves (called **sulci**). What do these wrinkles remind you of? (2)

4. Run your gloved hand over the surface of the cerebrum. How would you describe the surface? (3)

5. The cerebrum is composed of four major sections or lobes. Locate the following on the sheep brain:

   a. **Occipital lobe**, located in the back of the cerebrum, receives and interprets visual information from the eyes.
   b. **Temporal lobes**, located along the sides of the cerebrum, are involved in hearing and smell.
   c. **Frontal lobe**, located in front of the cerebrum, is involved in planning, organizing, problem solving, selective attention, personality, and a variety of "higher cognitive functions," including behavior and emotions.
   d. **Parietal lobes,** located in the middle of the cerebrum, are concerned with the perception of touch, pressure, temperature and pain.

Observations: External (outside) Bottom View

6. Turn the brain over to observe the bottom surface. Identify the **medulla, pons**, and **midbrain**. These three regions of the brain are commonly referred to as the brain stem.

7. Locate the **olfactory bulbs** on each hemisphere. They will be slightly smoother and a lighter shade than the surrounding tissue. The olfactory bulbs control the sense of smell. The nerves that once led to the nose are no longer present.

8. Locate the **optic chiasm**. The optic nerves from both eyes meet and cross at the optic chiasm. Images from the right eye are directed to the left side of the brain, while images from the left eye are sent to the right side of the brain for interpretation.

Part 2: Read and Follow steps 1-8

Observations: Internal (inside) View

1. Place the brain with the curved topside of the cerebrum facing up. Using the plastic knife, slice through the brain along the centerline. Start at the cerebrum and continue down through the cerebellum, spinal cord, medulla and pons. Carefully separate the two halves and lay them face up on the dissection pan. Which part of the brain was most difficult to cut through? (4)

2. Identify the **corpus callosum**. This bundle of neurons connects the two hemispheres of the brain, allowing coordination and communication between the two.

3. Locate the **medulla**, found directly under the cerebellum. This region of the brain controls vital body functions such as heartbeat and breathing.

4. The **pons** is located next to the medulla. Pons is the Latin word for bridge. The pons relays messages between the cerebrum and the cerebellum. It is responsible for breathing or respiration.

5. Next, locate a small sac-like structure called the **pituitary gland**. It might be difficult to see if it was damaged during the dissection. The pituitary gland produces important hormones, which are chemical substances that travel through the blood stream. This gland is often referred to as the "master gland." The pituitary gland controls body temperature and growth hormones, and plays a critical role in the body's ability to respond to the environment.

6. Examine the inside surface of the cerebellum. You will see a branching "tree" of white tissue that is surrounded by a slightly darker tissue. The white branching fibers are **white matter**, made up mostly of nerve axons. The darker, surrounding tissue is **gray matter**, which is a collection of nerve cell bodies.

7. Using the plastic knife, make a thin, horizontal slice through the cerebrum. Lift the flap of tissue and examine the underside. You should see both white and gray matter in the cerebrum as well.

8. Your teacher will provide you with 10 pins. Each pin will have a small, numbered flag attached to it. Using the diagrams provided, identify the ten brain structures listed below. Place each pin in the correct location. (Example: Pin # 1 should be placed in the Frontal Lobe.)

1. Frontal lobe
2. Temporal lobe
3. Parietal lobe
4. Occipital lobe
5. Cerebellum
6. Medulla
7. Pons
8. Corpus Callosum
9. Gray matter
10. White matter

Remember: Complete the **Student Observation Report** by answering the four questions and completing the Structure/Function chart.

Sheep Brain Lab
Student Observation Report

In the space below, answer the four questions found in the Sheep Brain Lab (look for the numbers in parenthesis)

1. _____
2. _____
3. _____
4. _____

Using the information provided in the Sheep Brain Observation Guide complete the chart below:

Structure	Function
Olfactory bulb	
Corpus Callosum	
Medulla	
Pons	
Pituitary Gland	
Ventricles	
Occipital Lobe	
Temporal Lobe	
Parietal Lobe	
Thalamus	
Pineal Gland	

Lesson 3.2

Brain in a Bag

Have you ever wondered what it would feel like to hold a human brain in your hands? What would its texture, weight and consistency be? Try this…

Materials:

- 1.5 cups (360 ml) instant potato flakes
- 2.5 cups (600 ml) hot water
- 2 cups (480 ml) clean sand
- 1 gallon ziplock bag

Directions:

Combine all of the ingredients in a gallon ziplock bag and mix thoroughly by kneading (gently squeezing) them with your hands. The bag should weigh about 3 lbs. (1.35 kg.), the weight of an average adult brain, and have the texture and feel of a real brain.

Note: Add a few drops of red food coloring to create a "pink" mixture. Remember the brain has a rich supply of blood vessels. Approximately 20% of all the blood pumped from the heart goes to the brain!

Lesson 3.3

Brain Puzzle

Color, Cut out and assemble (glue) and label the pieces of the brain puzzle
.

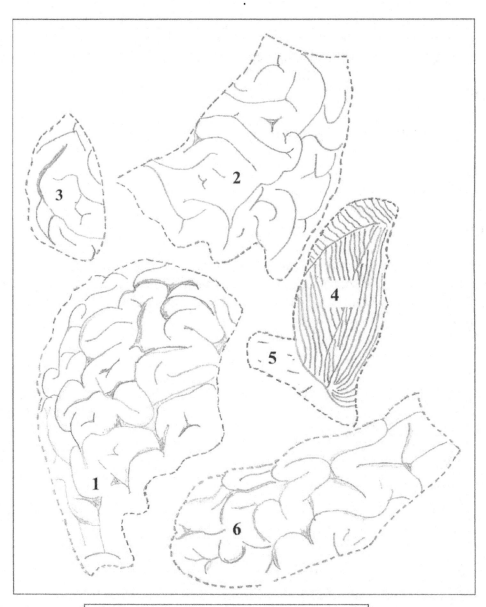

Color Code:

Frontal Lobe (1) - purple   Cerebellum (4)-pink
Parietal Lobe (2) - red   Brain Stem (5)-orange
Occipital Lobe (3) - green   Temporal Lobe (6) - blue

Lesson 3.4

Making Neurons from Clay

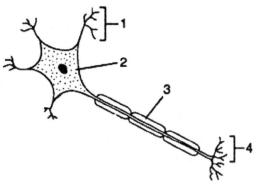

Purpose: The purpose of this lab is to demonstrate your understanding of neuron structure and neuron communication. You will use clay to create a model of a neuron. When you have completed your model, you will combine it with other students' models to create a neural network.

Materials:
5-6 different colors of modeling clay

4x6 inch index cards
Picture of neuron with labels

Procedure:

1. Use the clay provided to make a model of a neuron. The model must include dendrites, cell body, myelin sheath, axon and neurotransmitters.
2. Place the neuron model on the index card and label all five parts.
3. When instructed by the teacher, you organize into groups of 5-6 students.
4. With your group members, arrange the index cards (neurons) in a manner that would allow them to send an impulse or message across the desk.
5. Draw arrows on the index cards showing the direction the impulse will travel as it moves from neuron to neuron.
6. Label structures 1-4 on the neuron diagram in the box above.

Lesson 3.5

How Neurons Communicate

Everybody up! That's right, stand up and form a line or circle around the classroom. Each of you now represents a neuron. Stretch your arms out to the side. Your left hand and fingers represent the dendrites; your body is the cell body; your right arm is the axon and your right hand is the synaptic terminal. Make a fist with your right hand and insert the colored token between your folded fingers. The token represents the neurotransmitter that will stimulate the neighboring neuron.

Move apart so that you are slightly more than an arms length from the next person. Remember, the terminal end of an axon does not touch the dendrites of the neighboring neuron. The "gap" between the two neurons is called the synapse. When your teacher says, "start", the first student will pass their neurotransmitter (token) into the left hand of the adjacent student. Once the message is received, the second student will pass **their token** or neurotransmitter into the hand of the person next to them, until the last token in line is transferred.

Remember that each neuron will pass its own neurotransmitter to the next neuron. Each neuron has its own neurotransmitter!

Using a stopwatch, measure how many seconds it takes for the message to get from the first neuron to the last. Measure the distance from the first to the last neuron in meters. Calculate the speed, Distance ÷ Time. Your answer should be in meters per second.

Axon size does affect axon speed. In the smallest axons, impulses crawl at a slothful 1 mph. They zoom through the largest axons at 270 mph.

Tips for Implementing Lessons

Chapter Three

Lesson 3.1 – Sheep Brain Lab

Main Idea: In learning about the human brain, it is important for students to have an opportunity to dissect, describe and identify the major structures of a mammalian brain. The sheep brain dissection is relatively simple and inexpensive. This engaging activity enhances the understanding of, and the appreciation for, the human brain.

Suggestions:

- Sheep brain specimens can be ordered from area biological supply companies (http://www.enasco.com/product/LS01152MH).

- To reduce cost, students can work in groups of 4-6.

- Collaborate with science teachers on staff when planning the sheep brain lab.

- Flag pins can by made by attaching a piece of scotch tape to the top of large straight pins. Number the pins 1-10.

- An online guide for the sheep brain dissection can be found at: http://academic.uofs.edu/department/psych/sheep.

- Additional images to assist students in locating specific structures in the sheep brain, can be found at : http://www.gwc.maricopa.edu/class/bio201/brain/brshpx.htm

Lesson 3.2 – Brain in a Bag

Main Idea: Students are naturally curious about the size, weight and volume of the brain. This activity satisfies that curiosity and allows them to experience the brain's texture, weight and consistency.

Suggestions:

- This activity can be done as a demonstration or with students in groups of 2-4.

- After the material as been kneaded in the bags, students can place it on a placemat and experiment with sculpting it into a brain. Encourage them to sculpt the following structures: right and left cerebral hemispheres, brain stem, sulci and gyri.

Lesson 3.3 – Brain Puzzle
Main Idea: Students will learn the location and function of major brain structures.

Suggestions:

- After students cut out and assembled the brain puzzle, they should paste it onto an 8.5" x 11" sheet of paper. Next, have students label and color the six brain structures.

- Encourage students to research the primary function of each brain structure and record this information on the brain puzzle.

Lesson 3.4 – Making Neurons from Clay
Main Idea: Students will build a clay model, demonstrating their understanding of neuron structure and function. Understanding neuron structure will allow them to comprehend how the brain learns and grows with experience, effort and practice.

Suggestions:

- Read and share with students the information found in the section titled "Neural Networks Are Knowledge."

- Use the instructions found in "Demonstrating the Parts of a Neuron" to teach and review the parts of a neuron.

- Emphasize that through effort and practice, the brain will grow and expand its neural networks (sprout new dendrites). Explain that learning occurs as new and stronger connections are made between neurons. We now know that learning creates a *physical change* in the brain.

- Remind students that when a brain is bored and unchallenged, neural networks shrink, and gray matter disappears.

Lesson 3.5 – How Neurons Communicate
Main Idea: When neural networks fire, neurons communicate with each other. Focused effort and practice can increase the speed and efficiency of neural communication.

Suggestions:

- You can use poker chips for the colored tokens.

- Provide an opportunity for students to research the function of some common neurotransmitters, such as dopamine and serotonin.

- Several interactive websites are available online to expand student understanding of neuron structure and function.

Step 3

Present evidence of neuroplasticity. Discover the effect of an enriched environment on neural networks. Inspire effort & practice.

Review and summarize current, credible research in the area of neuroplasticity, confirming that intelligence is malleable, and that the brain is plastic – capable of changing itself, based on life's experiences. Share inspirational, personal stories that document the effects of practice and effort. Illustrate how an enriched environment shapes the human brain.

Chapter Four

"The bottom line is that experience changes the physiological structure and operation of our brains."

- Renate and Geoffrey Caine

-

Brain Plasticity

Searching for Evidence

Out of curiosity, I pulled a textbook off my bookshelf; one purchased my first year in college – *Fundamental Concepts of Modern Biology,* copyrighted 1971. On page 348, I found what I was looking for, a passage describing the characteristics of a neuron. It read:

Neurons do not divide during growth or after injury. An individual is born with all the neurons he will ever have and these remain with him throughout life. When a neuron is destroyed, it is not replaced by another.

As I sifted through my collection of science books, I discovered the **myth** of the "fixed number of neurons" and the story of the "immutable brain" described repeatedly. Even in the current biology textbooks, there was no mention of brain plasticity or neurogenesis. I found this a surprising fact, considering that in the early sixties, investigators were already seriously speculating that environmental influences might be capable of altering brain structure. Despite growing evidence, the scientific community persisted in its teaching, that the adult brain does not create new brain cells - that our supply of neurons steadily diminishes throughout our lives, never to be replenished. It appears that misconceptions in science are sometimes as difficult to discredit as old wives' tales. Do you still believe that it takes chewing gum seven years to pass through the digestive system, and that you only use 10% of your brain?

Most school districts have a ten-year book adoption cycle. Because much of the significant research related to neuroplasticity has been conducted over the past decade, it is possible that it could be another ten years before news of this research finds its way into classroom science books. Can we afford to wait for textbook publishers to deliver the news? How important is it for teachers, parents, and students to know and understand that effort, practice, and an enriched environment impact brain structure and intelligence? Shouldn't we inform all students that **"Smart is something you get, not something you are"?**

A Timeline of Discovery – Debunking the Myth

How do we know that the brain is plastic, that it can create new neurons, a process known as neurogenesis? What evidence do we have that the brain is shaped and sculpted by our experiences? Let's review a timeline of discovery. For the sake of brevity, I have included only key discoveries.

18th century –Italian anatomist, Michele Malacarne, found differences between the brains of differentially trained animals.

1949 – Donald Hebb published his book, *The Organization.* A central principle of his theory was that experience modifies the brain. A few years before publishing his book, Hebb reported on the first experiment that systematically compared the *problem solving ability* of rats reared in different conditions. Hebb reared two litters of rats at home as pets. These rats were permitted to roam freely throughout the house, spending little time in their cages. Hebb discovered that these pet rats scored far better than laboratory-reared rats when challenged to find their way through a maze. He did not compare the brains of the rats in his experiment, and he did not speculate on the impact that enriched early experiences might have on brain anatomy, but he did acknowledge this: *"The richer experience of the pet group during development made them better able to profit by new experiences at maturity."*

1964 – E.L. Bennet said that rats that were better at learning mazes had higher ACh (a neurotransmitter) activity than those who were not good at learning mazes. Later, research found that stimulation and training, in fact, increased levels of ACh.

1965 – Marian Diamond demonstrated with rat studies, that environmental enrichment could modify structural components of the rat brain at any age. She documented that the cerebral cortex, the area associated with higher thinking skills, is more receptive than other regions of the brain to environmental enrichment. She also noted that enriched environments had consequences for animal behaviors.

1983 – Fernando Nottebohm studied songbirds, and reported the discovery of new neurons (neurogenesis) in adult canaries as they learned new songs each season. **Dr. Nottebohm's lab was the first to provide irrefutable evidence that new nerve cells are constantly born in an adult vertebrate brain, where they replace older cells of the same kind that have died.**

1990 – Elizabeth Gould provided scientific evidence that new neurons are produced in the hippocampus of adult rats and primates.

1998 – Peter Eriksson and Fred Gage published results in the Nov.1, 1998 issue of *Nature Medicine,* showing that new cells were generated in the brains of terminal cancer patients who had undergone a diagnostic procedure that labels actively dividing cells. Upon the patients' death, their brains were examined by Gage and Eriksson. They discovered that, contrary to prior belief, brain cells in adult humans do multiply. All of the brains examined showed evidence of new mature neurons. **This was the first evidence for neurogenesis in the adult human brain, and it was seen in indiviuals in their fifties and seventies. The implication - human beings are capable of growing new nerve cells throughout life.** Fred Gage was quoted as saying, after the discovery,
" The current finding brings us an important step closer to thinking that we have more control over our own brain capacity then we ever thought possible."

2002 – Henriette van Praag and Fred Gage used a retrovirus that makes the cells it infects appear florescent green. Because this retrovirus only attaches to neurons undergoing cell division, they could detect the presences of new neurons. Using this technique, the team confirmed a 15% increase of new neurons in the hippocampus of rats reared in an enriched environment. In addition, for the first time, scientists observed that new neurons produced in the hippocampus and olfactory bulb of rats become functional members of the brain network, forging new connections and firing like other neurons.

> *"What we have going on here is a periodic insertion of a new, young brain cell within the context of the older cells in the environment. This gives a self-renewal property to the structure, by adding these new, more malleable cells."*
> *Fred Gage*

What began with a few pet rats, running free in a house, and a scientist's curiosity about a small bird's ability to learn new songs, caused a paradigm shift in neuroscience. We now know that neurogenesis is a reality in the adult brain, that many of these new neurons survive and integrate themselves into the functioning brain, suggesting the potential for a brain that can heal itself.

Researchers are now investigating the processes that might promote or inhibit neurogenesis. Compiled evidence shows that exercise is good for the brain. Mice that used a running wheel had about twice as many new hippocampal neurons as mice that did not exercise (Gage 1999). In addition, experiments using antidepressant therapy found that it stimulates neurogenesis in adult animals. Not so surprising, is the news that stress seems to work against the production of new brain cells (Karten 2005).

A key discovery we should NOT overlook is this; to live and become part of the working brain, a new neuron needs more than just nutrients and oxygen. It must also establish connections with other surrounding neurons. Without these connections, new neurons wither and die. There is a direct correlation between learning (making new connections) and new neuron survival rate. **The more we learn, the more connections we make, the more new neurons we get to keep!**

Neuroscience for Kids - A Message of Hope

Hope is much more than just a cheery outlook; it plays a powerful role in shaping our decisions and our lives. C.R. Snyder, a University of Kansas psychologist, defines hope as "believing you have both the will and the way to accomplish your goals, whatever they may be." Moreover, he knows that hope can make all the difference (Snyder 1994). His research documents that college students with high levels of hope, work harder and think of alternative strategies when they are struggling with grades. He discovered that hope was a better predictor of the first-semester grades than were student SAT scores. Having hope means, that one is less likely to give up when facing difficulties and setbacks. Hopeful individuals can better maneuver through life's challenges in pursuit of their dreams.

> *"Students with high hope set themselves higher goals and know how to work hard to attain them. When you compare students of equal intellectual aptitude on their academic achievements, what sets them part is hope."*
>
> *C.R. Snyder*

The following are stories and lessons that illustrate the amazing plasticity of the human brain. They reveal new and exciting secrets about how the brain learns and responds to life's experiences, and they help to explain the impact of attention, effort, and practice on brain structure. I discovered that sharing these stories with my seventh grade students transformed their motivation to learn. I hope that you will read and share these stories with your students, as they will deliver a powerful message of hope.

If you embrace new challenges, give your best effort and practice, you will grow in intelligence. We all have the potential to grow a better brain.

J.M.B.

Lesson 4.1
The Power of the Brain to Change

She was a young girl about fourteen, accompanying her father on his rounds at the hospital, when she first laid eyes on the gleaming, wrinkled mass. Peering into the hospital room, she saw four doctors huddled around the intriguing mound of tissue, a human brain, as it lay on a small square table. Most teens would have been horrified by such a sight, but not Marian. She remembers saying to herself, "That mass used to think! How can living cells – well, previously living cells – produce ideas?" At fourteen, she had an experience that would shape the rest of her life.

A long held belief was that once we reached adulthood, we only lost neurons and nerve cell connections; we did not gain them. Neuroscientists believed that the neurons in the brain were fixed early in life. They believed that the circuits of the adult brain were unchangeable, fixed in form and function. Many neuroscientists described the adult brain as being "hardwired." This would suggest that with regard to intelligence, we are pretty much stuck with what we have … not a very uplifting thought.

Thanks to over twenty years of research, we now know that the brain is **not** fixed, but can and does change, grow, and remodel itself. The human brain exhibits amazing plasticity. **Plasticity** is the lifelong ability of the brain to reorganize neural pathways based on new experiences. Research has revealed that the brain continues changing and adjusting, until it ceases to be alive.

It is now clear that genetics is not the only factor that shapes the brain. The characteristics of a person's environment, their experiences, and their actions play a key role in influencing plasticity and shaping the brain.

Dr. Marian Diamond, Professor of Anatomy at the University of California in Berkeley, has devoted over thirty years to the study of how enriched environments can improve brain size and performance. She conducted experiments on rats to learn about the effects of environment on neurons, dendrites, and intelligence (Diamond 1988). Rats were exposed to three different environments, each with different levels of stimulation.

Below is a description of the three experimental groups:

Group 1: For the enriched environment, the 12 rats lived together in a large cage and were provided 5-6 objects to explore and climb upon (e.g., wheels, ladders, small mazes). The objects were changed two to three times a week to provide newness and challenge. This group had plenty of friends and toys to enjoy.

Group 2: For the standard environment, the animals were housed three to a small cage with no exploratory objects. The standard environment provided fewer friends and no toys to enjoy.

Group 3: For the impoverished environment, one animal remained alone in a small cage with no exploratory objects. Imagine no friends and no toys to play with!

The Results:

After 30 days, researchers carefully examined brain tissue from all three groups. Results indicated clearly that the cortex from the enriched group had increased in thickness compared with the group living in standard conditions, whereas, the brains from the impoverished group decreased compared to the standard.

As the rats in **Group 1** interacted with each other and challenged themselves on the many toys provided, their brains underwent a physical change. This rich environment stimulated the rats' neurons, causing them to fire more frequently. As a result, they **grew more dendrites** in the cerebral cortex, the part of the brain where higher thinking occurs. This group also demonstrated greater ability to maneuver mazes than did the rats raised in the impoverished environment.

The rats in **Group 2** did not exhibit any growth in the cerebral cortex. This group did not demonstrate an improved ability to maneuver the mazes.

The rats in **Group 3** actually *lost* thickness in the cerebral cortex and had more difficulty maneuvering the mazes. The conclusion is that when neurons do not receive stimulation, they shrink. Neuroscientists sometimes refer to this as the "use it or lose it" phenomena.

In later experiments, conditions were modified in an attempt to establish the major factors that created the changes in the cerebral cortex of the rats. Researchers wonded if it was the social conditions (friends) or the stimulus objects (toys) that produced the changes.

The new conditions included one rat living alone in the large enrichment cage with the objects that were changed several times each week. Despite the engaging toys, the cortex of these rats did not show a significant change. In another group, 12 rats living together in the large cage without the stimulus objects did not show as great an effect as 12 rats living together with the stimulus objects. In other words, the combination of social conditions (friends) and the frequent exposure to new stimulus objects (challenges) was necessary for the rats to gain the full effect of the enriched environment. The rats needed both friends and stimulating challenges to grow their brains.

Dr. Diamond, in her book *Magic Trees of the Mind* said, "A brain impoverished of any stimulation can certainly atrophy, but one in an 'enriched' environment will send out fresh branches of dendrites that take in new information and axons that transmit signals. The cortex will grow or shrink relative to its use," she affirmed, "just like a muscle."

Many experiments have shown that experience changes the wiring and structure in the brain. Enriched and challenging environments make neurons more active, producing extensive new branching. Research confirms that when the brain is stimulated and challenged it will grow in intelligence. The more connections you make… the more pathways to success you create!

Dr. Marian Diamond, now in her eighties, is a distinguished professor of Integrative Biology at University of California at Berkeley. She is widely recognized as one of the world's foremost experts on experience-dependent structural changes in the brain – on how learning influences neural growth.

Student Reflection:

1. Create a sequence of cartoon pictures, describing Dr. Marian Diamond's research. What did she discover about the relationship between environment and intelligence?

Lesson 4.2

Dr. Paul Bach-y-Rita

A Father's Inspiration

Picture an old man as he crawls around the family garden like an animal on all fours. His paralyzed face reveals a mouth that hangs at an awkward slant, with drool running out of its corners. "Fetch that marble," the old man's son shouts, as he rolls it across the ground, "come on, you can do it." The neighbors peer over the fence, looking on in horror.

Paul Bach-y-Rita was born to Anne Hymann and Pedro Bach-y-Rita on April 4, 1934. Much like his father, Paul was spirited, free-willed, adventurous, and determined. He began studying science while a student at the Bronx High School in New York, where he proved to be an enthusiastic learner, graduating from high school at fifteen and from Mexico City College (now the University of the Americas in Puebla) at the age of seventeen. After college graduation, Paul decided to attend medical school, but hungry for adventure, he quit after his first year and embarked on a series of odd jobs.

Paul worked as a salmon and shrimp fisherman, trained as a massage therapist, and even taught anatomy and physiology to blind veterans in a massage therapy program. Working with the blind sparked an interest in studying vision, resulting in Paul Bach-y-Rita's return to medical school. By the time he was 37, he would be a full professor at the Smith-Kettleward Institute of Visual Sciences in San Francisco.

Sometimes a tragic event can change the direction of one's life. For Paul Bach-y-Rita, that tragic event occurred in 1958, when his father, 68-year-old Pedro Bach-y-Rita experienced a massive stroke that paralyzed his face, half of his body, and left him unable to speak. Doctors told Paul and his brother, George, that their father had no hope for recovery, and that he should be moved to a skilled nursing home, where he would be institutionalized for the rest of his life.

Determined to help George (a medical student at the time) took his father, back to Mexico to live with him and enrolled him in a four-week stroke rehabilitation program. Sadly, it produced little improvement. Pedro still could not care for his basic needs; someone still had to assist by giving him a shower, as well as helping him onto and off the toilet. Confined to a wheelchair, Pedro was unable to speak. Each day he grew more helpless and more depressed.

In 1958, at the time of Pedro Bach-y-Rita's stroke, neuroscientists held the belief that most brain damage was irreversible – that once nerve cells were destroyed, their functions were lost forever. Doctors believed that if a stroke resulted in paralysis or loss of brain function for more than a few weeks, the damage was permanent. Rehabilitation doctors and specialists offered little hope for recovery after the typical four-week rehabilitation program ended.

George Bach-y-Rita was certainly not an expert in stroke rehabilitation, but he rejected the pessimistic outlook for his father. Undeterred by professionals in the field, George broke all of the usual rules, and developed a new rehabilitation program with amazing results!

George told his father, "You started off crawling; you are going to have to crawl again for a while." He got kneepads for his dad, put them on him, and then helped lift him up on all fours. At first, the process was very difficult; his dad's arms and legs were weak, and he could not support himself. George would place Pedro's weak side up against the wall where his dad would inch along, struggling to make the slightest forward progress.

Believing in the healing power of nature, George carried his father outside into the garden where the crawling practice continued. Imagine what the neighbors thought! The two men would play games– practicing the skills of picking up coins, and of rolling and retrieving marbles – with Pedro always using the weaker right side of his body as much as possible. The results of all this hard work, practice, and determination were nothing short of a miracle.

Still back in California, Paul Bach-y-Rita marveled at the reports of his father's progress. George described to his brother how their father had first crawled, later stood, and ultimately walked again. At the end of one year, his father's recovery was so complete that Pedro Bach-y-Rita returned to his full-time teaching job at City College in New York. A widower, he remarried, took a second job, and worked until he retired at age seventy-two. Seven years after suffering his massive stroke, he was visiting friends in Bogotá, Colombia, where he was mountain climbing. At nine thousand feet, he had a heart attack and died.

After his death, Pedro's body was returned to San Francisco, where Dr. Mary Aguilar performed a routine autopsy to determine the cause of death. Thin slices of the brain were prepared and examined . . . the findings were an absolute shock! **Ninety-seven percent of the nerves that run from the cerebral cortex to the spine had been destroyed!** The huge lesion in his brain (a result of the stroke) had never healed; yet amazingly Pedro had somehow fully recovered the brain's lost functions. Such massive damage should have, seemingly, made Pedro's rehabilitation impossible. How could medical doctors account for his astonishing recovery?

Paul Bach-y-Rita later explained, "I knew it meant that somehow his brain had totally reorganized itself because of the work he did with my brother George. We didn't know how remarkable his recovery was until that moment, because there were no brain scans in those days. When people did recover, we tended to assume that there really hadn't been much damage in the first place."

Inspired by his father's miraculous recovery, Paul Bach-y-Rita left his promising career in the field of eye movements, and completed a residency in neurology rehabilitation medicine. He wanted to study and help stroke patients like his father. He was the first of his generation of neuroscientists to understand that the human brain is plastic, and that it can rewire and reshape itself. Armed with this new evidence, he went on to develop many new devices that would assist stroke patients and handicapped individuals.

Dr. Paul Bach-y-Rita was a pioneer in the field of neuroplasticity; he believed in the power of the brain to change throughout an individual's lifetime. His experience with his father, and years of careful research, confirmed his beliefs. During therapy sessions, when his patients' progress would slow or stop, he would push them to continue. What he discovered was that, despite the lack of outward physical improvement, internal changes continued to rewire the brain. If patients continued with their efforts, they would typically experience a break-through, and progress would continue. He provided evidence that neuroplasticity is a not a myth, but a powerful reality. Doctors Paul and George Bach-y-Rita and their father, Pedro Bach-y-Rita, delivered a powerful message about the plasticity of the human brain. It was a powerful message filled with **HOPE**.

Student Reflection:

1. After reading the story about Pedro Bach-y-Rita, what suggestions would you give someone recovering from a stroke?

Lesson 4.3

Living With Half a Brain

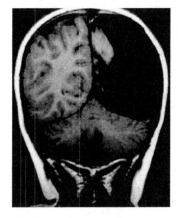

He saw confirming evidence that the brain was deteriorating and parts of it were dying. He worked systematically, moving from the front towards the back of the brain. Tissue that could not be removed in chunks was suctioned through a pipe. He worked meticulously until the right side of Cameron's skull was empty.

The first three years of Cameron Mott's life were textbook normal. She was an active, bright, engaging little girl. Blonde curls framed her little face and sparkling blue eyes. She was the picture of good health, before the first storm hit.

At three years of age, Cameron was diagnosed with a rare and deadly brain disorder, Rasmussen's Encephalitis, a debilitating condition that affects less than one in a thousand children.

This degenerative disease produces a storm of electrical surges in the brain, causing repeated epileptic seizures. By the age of six, Cameron was experiencing as many as fifteen seizures per day. Suddenly without warning, her muscles tensed and stiffened, as she collapsed to the floor. Because her fits were unpredictable, Cameron wore a helmet to protect her from the constant threat of head injury. The disease was slowly eating away at her brain, robbing her of any chance of a normal life. As the disease spread through Cameron's right hemisphere, it affected the opposite side of her body, gradually paralyzing her left hand and leg. Medications had little or no impact.

Left untreated, Cameron's disease would continue to eat away at the remaining healthy brain tissue, leading to brain damage and a severely handicapped condition. The only cure would be a hemispherectomy, a radical operation to remove the diseased right half of her brain. Dr. George Jallo, a neurosurgeon at The John Hopkins Children's Center in Baltimore, performed the operation. For ten hours, Cameron lay stretched out on the operating table as Dr. Jallo slowly and carefully cut, suctioned, and removed nearly one-half of her brain.

The procedure began as Dr. Jallo gently removed the front section of the skull, lifting the dura mater exposing the diseased tissue underneath. The dura mater, which is normally translucent, was tough, opaque and showed signs of inflammation. He saw confirming evidence that the brain was deteriorating, and that parts of it were dying. He worked systematically and meticulously to remove the diseased brain tissue, until the right side of Cameron's skull was empty. In a critical last step, he left a small piece of the brain to protect the fragile area surrounding Cameron's spinal cord and then severed the corpus callosum, the band of fibers located deep within the brain that connects the two halves.

The open cavity on the right side of Cameron's head would quickly fill with cerebral spinal fluid, at a rate of one teaspoonful every five minutes. For the next 48 hours, Cameron's head must be kept completely still so the remaining left half of her brain would not be dislodged.

After years of debilitating seizures, her journey towards recovery was under way. Her brain quickly began to recreate itself, forming new connections between neurons to replace lost ones. It reorganized itself, transferring skills normally undertaken by one-half of the brain to the other. Initially Cameron could not move her left side, but rapidly she gained strength and was able to stand and bear weight. Miraculously, after only ten days, she walked out of the hospital unaided, to start a new life. She returned to school, dance lessons, and to a life free of seizures and full of promise.

Each day brought new evidence that Cameron's brain was recovering. With courage and determination, she made extraordinary progress. She was living proof, that it is not the number of neurons that make the human brain work so brilliantly, but rather the number of connections between neurons, connections that will form when the brain is challenged. As new neural connections are made, new networks form and the brain's power grows.

Children like Cameron, who have undergone a radical hemispherectomy, demonstrate the amazing plasticity of the human brain. They inspire us with their effort and determination as they aim to grow their brain!

Lesson 4.4

My Stroke of Insight

A Brain Scientist's Personal Journey to Recover Her Brain

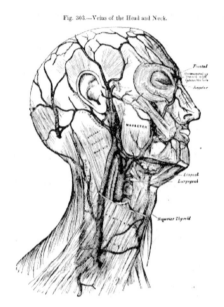

Fig. 303.—Veins of the Head and Neck.

Jill was sleeping peacefully, unaware that a life-changing event was underway…Within her skull, pressure was building inside a vein buried deep in her brain. As the pressure grew, the vein expanded like a balloon, until at last it split, spilling a large volume of blood over the left hemisphere of her brain.

The result would be devastating. While blood is a life-giving fluid to all other cells of the body, it is a toxin, a poison to neurons. As blood made direct contact with Jill's brain cells, it killed them, leaving a pathway of destruction. When Jill awoke to her alarm at 7:00 a.m. on December 10, 1996, she slowly began to realize that her brain, body and life would never be the same. On this day, Dr. Jill Bolte Taylor, a professor of neuroanatomy, would not deliver a lecture on brain anatomy to her students, but instead would arrive at Massachusetts General Hospital emergency ward as a stroke patient.

Jill Bolte Taylor grew up in Terre Haute, Indiana. She became interested in studying the human brain at an early age, inspired by an older brother diagnosed with schizophrenia. Jill grew up wanting to understand and learn more about this serious mental illness. At the University of Indiana in Bloomington, she studied physiological psychology and human biology, learning all she could about how the brain works. After finishing her undergraduate degree, Jill spent the next six years at Indiana State

University where her research specialty was neuroanatomy. In 1991, she received her doctorate and accepted a research position at Harvard Medical School in the department of Neuroscience.

Jill was thirty-seven years old and a rising star in the field of brain science when she experienced a massive stoke on the left side of her brain. The result of a rare genetic disease, she would find herself unable to talk, walk, write, or recall any details of her life. Suddenly, the language and calculating centers in her left hemisphere shut down. Her ability to process information was severely limited. As Jill described it, "Even though my brain remained lined with filing cabinets, it was as if all the drawers had been slammed shut and the cabinets pushed just beyond my reach. I was saddened that perhaps those portions of my mind were now lost forever."

The first warning sign Jill experienced that morning had been the intense, sharp pain she felt behind her left eye. The early morning light aggravated the throbbing pain and led her to close the blinds. Unaware she was experiencing a stroke Jill lifted herself onto her "cardio-glider" and began to exercise. As she started moving, she experienced the sensation that her brain and body were oddly disconnected. Her movements were no longer smooth and coordinated but jerky, and she struggled to keep her balance.

By the end of the day, Jill would be in the hospital curled in a fetal position and unable to hear anything other than the pounding rhythm of her own heartbeat. Two weeks later, she would undergo major brain surgery to remove the golf-ball-sized blood clot blocking her brain's ability to transmit information. Now it was time to re-teach her damaged brain to control such actions as moving her body, walking, talking, writing, and doing math.

Because Jill was a trained neuroanatomist, she had an advantage. She understood and **believed** in the plasticity of the brain. Years of research and study had provided evidence of the brain's ability to repair, replace, and retain its neural circuitry. Understanding and firmly believing in the **resiliency** of her brain, Jill – with the help of her mother and medical team – developed a "roadmap" for her recovery.

Jill learned to break every new task down into smaller and simpler steps. She learned to rock back and forth in her bed and eventually roll over before she could sit up. Jill knew that with effort and determined focus, new dendrite connections would sprout, and new neural networks would flourish. Practice and repetition would increase the speed and smoothness of her thoughts and movements. In her book, *My Stroke of Insight*, Dr. Taylor described how effort and focused attention were keys to her recovery.

> *"By celebrating my achievements every day, I stayed focused on how well I was doing. I made the choice that it didn't matter if I could walk, talk, or even know my name. If all I was doing was breathing, then we (Jill & her mom) celebrated that I was alive— and we breathed together. If I stumbled, then we could celebrate when I was upright. If I was drooling, we celebrated swallowing. It would have been really easy, a thousand times a day, to feel as though I was less than who I was before. I had after all, lost my mind and therefore had legitimate reason to feel sorry for myself."*

It took **eight years** for Jill to recover completely— eight years of intense effort, focus, and practice. An awareness of her body's need for rest and sleep also produced amazing results. Ultimately, though, it was her "growth mindset" that allowed Jill to embrace the difficult challenges during her long recovery. Read this excerpt from her book *My Stroke of Insight*. Can you detect the "growth mindset"?

> *"Paying attention to what someone was saying took an enormous amount of effort, and I found it to be tiring. First, I had to pay attention with my eyes and ears, neither of which were working normally. My brain had to capture the sound and then match that sound up with a specific lip movement. Then, I had to search and see if there was any meaning for those combinations of sounds stored anywhere in my wounded brain. The effort it took for me to pay attention to what someone was saying was like the effort it takes to pay attention to someone who is speaking on a cell phone with a bad connection. It took a tremendous amount of willingness and determination on my part, and infinite patience on the part of the speaker."*

Although much of the old Jill disappeared on that December morning, she soon realized that she now had the opportunity to rebuild and remodel her brain and her life. While the badly damaged left hemisphere would need to be retrained and rewired, she challenged herself to explore, expand and develop her right hemisphere. The once driven, rational, detail-oriented, left-brained Jill Bolte Taylor would recover, but she would be a changed person.

Today, Jill is quick to say that the stroke was the best thing that could have happened to her. Like others who possess the "growth mindset," she saw opportunities for growth when faced with the difficult challenge of recovery. As the left side of her brain shut down, she uncovered feelings of well-being and peace in the right hemisphere, causing her to be less judgmental and more compassionate. Her mistakes or the mistakes of others would no longer haunt or demoralize her. Forgiving herself and forgiving others would become a choice she could always make.

Currently, Jill is a neuroanatomist at Indiana University School of Medicine in Indianapolis and the consulting neuroanatomist for the Midwest Proton Radiotherapy Institute. In addition, she is a national spokesperson for the mentally ill at the Harvard Brain Tissue Resource Center. As their spokesperson, she encourages members of her audience to donate their brain to the Harvard Brain Bank for research purposes. "Don't worry though," she says, "we can wait until you are done with it!" In 2006, she wrote and published, *My Stroke of Insight*, a book in which she shares her inspiring story and unique perspective on the brain and its amazing capacity for recovery. By sharing her personal journey, she reaffirms that when we embrace challenges, give our best effort, and practice often, we can and will grow our brain and increase our intelligence.

Lesson 4.5

Dr. Merzenich's Monkey Business

Your brain is like a powerful car just waiting to be driven, and **you** hold the key. In the case of your brain, the key is **attention**.

Paying attention harnesses the brain's phenomenal power to do its work of transformation – of growing itself to create the skills and knowledge you need.

Neurologist Dr. Mike Merzenich has been studying the powers of the brain for a long time, and he has shown the dramatic results of paying attention through his experiments with monkeys (Merzenich 1998). He wanted to see if paying attention was necessary to create changes in the brain's structure.

For his experiment, the doctor used a device that tapped the monkeys' fingers for one hundred minutes (a little over an hour and a half) a day for six weeks. He also put headphones on the monkeys so they could hear certain sounds in addition to feeling the finger tapping. Then, he divided the animals into two groups.

Group A:

Dr. Merzenich taught these monkeys to pay attention to the finger tapping. If the monkeys responded to a change in the rhythm of the tapping, they were rewarded with a sip of juice.

Group B:

Dr. Merzenich taught these monkeys to pay attention to the sounds from the headphones. If the monkeys responded to a change in the sound, they got their reward – a sip of juice.

After six weeks, Dr. Merzenich and his colleagues compared the monkeys' brains. It is important to remember, that monkeys in both groups had the exact same physical experience- sounds coming from the headphones and tapping on the fingers. The only factor that made one monkey different from another was what it **paid attention** to.

Group A:

The monkeys who learned to pay attention to the finger tapping for their reward, showed a dramatic increase in the brain region that responds to sensory input from the fingers. Paying careful attention to the tapping caused that specific part of the brain to expand. The brain region handling auditory sensation (sound) did not grow or expand in this group.

Group B:

The monkeys focusing on the headphone sounds for their reward showed an expansion of the brain's region that handles sound. In their case, the region of the brain that takes data from the fingers was unchanged.

The Conclusion:

These results have a clear application for students. The message is this: when you focus your attention on something, the brain responds and begins to alter its physical structure. However, if you are not paying attention to something, the brain interprets your lack of interest as a signal to remain unchanged. It does not begin the work of transformation that brings new and expanded skills and knowledge to its master.

Both **attention** and **repetitive practice** are necessary to generate changes in the structure of the brain. The brain does not make changes without focused attention, effort and practice. To unleash the power of a car, the driver must turn on the key, and practice driving!

Lesson 4.6

Tips to Help Students Focus

& Pay Attention

It is easy to get distracted or lose interest when lessons get hard, or when you find them boring. Even when you are interested in the teacher's instruction, there always seems to be something else to grab your attention.

Have you ever found yourself preparing to copy the agenda and start your warm-up, when suddenly the kid next to you breaks into a drum solo, madly tapping pencils on the desk? Or, one of your friends across the room passes you a juicy note. You probably face many distractions during the school day. At home, other distractions vie for your attention: television, video games, the internet, and phone calls from friends. How is a person to stay focused?

Neuroscientists agree that when it comes to learning, there is no substitute for paying attention. For the brain to acquire new information and process it, a person must *first* pay attention. So, what can you do to help improve your concentration and strengthen your ability to stay focused?

Sam Horn, an award winning speaker and author, offers these five FOCUS tips. You might use one or more of these tips the next time you find your attention wandering…

F= "Five More" Rule

Athletes have to build strength and stamina by pushing past the point of exhaustion. They tell themselves, "Just run *five* more minutes, do *five* more repetitions, do *five* more push-ups, etc." You can build up *mental stamina* in much the same way, by pushing past the point of frustration or boredom. Tell yourself, "I will do just five more math problems, read five more pages, or answer five more questions." Research shows that by doing this, you can *stretch your attention span* and build mental endurance. Frequently, if you will "just do five more" you will find that you can push past your point of frustration, refocus your attention, and keep going and going…

O = One at a Time

Are you feeling overwhelmed? Math, science, English, history, reading, band, athletics – how are you going to keep up with all of that? Remember, don't try to tackle everything at once. Make a to-do list. Try to list things in order of importance. Now, tell yourself, "I am going to start with number one on the list, and forget about everything else for now. From 4:30- 5:00, I am going to study my Greek and Latin root words, because I have a quiz tomorrow. Assign your brain a *single* task, and give it start and stop times. When the first task on your list is complete, cross it off the list, and reward yourself by relaxing a little.

C = Conquer Procrastination

"In a moment of decision, the best thing you can do is the right thing to do. The worst thing you can do is nothing."
Theodore Roosevelt

The next time you are about to postpone (put off) a responsibility (i.e. homework, studying for a test, writing a research paper), ask yourself these three questions:

1. Do I have to do this eventually?
2. Do I want it done so that I can stop worrying about it?
3. Will it be any easier to do later?

Often, asking these three questions helps you come face to face with the fact that:

- this task is not going to go away

- delaying it will only add to your guilt and worry

- the task will not get easier, and might actually be more difficult the longer you put it off.

"Procrastination is the grave in which opportunity is buried."
Author Unknown

When in doubt, get started. Start with baby steps if you have to, but do not procrastinate!

U = Use Your Hands as Blinkers

Have you ever wondered why some horses wear blinkers? You know, this is the headgear that keeps a horse from looking left or right. (Blinkers are sometimes called blinders.) These keep the horse focused on what is in front of it. They are frequently used in situations where there may be distractions, such as during a parade.

Try this…cup your hands around your eyes (like blinkers), so that you see only what is directly in front of you. The idea is to block out all the surrounding visual distractions. What you cannot see, cannot distract you! The next time you are reading, and need to concentrate on the material, put on your blinkers. Cup your hands around your eyes, and train your brain to focus on the task *in front of your face.*

If you use this tip regularly, you can condition your brain to switch to "one track" and to concentrate whenever you put on your blinkers. Your brain will zoom in like a telephoto lens, focusing on the task in front of you!

S = See, As if For the First or Last Time.

This is an interesting concept. Have you heard the expression, "running around like a chicken with its head cut off"? Do you know what the expression means? Gross as it may sound, a chicken frequently will continue to run around for a few minutes after it has been decapitated (had its head chopped off). When people run around mindlessly, not paying attention to their surroundings, we sometimes compare them to headless chickens.

Remember, the brain cannot learn when you are running around mindlessly. Stop and study details in your surroundings. Look at things *as if seeing them for the first time.* Use all of your senses to take in the moment. Wake up your eyes! Study pictures, stories, and words carefully. **Focus! Stop taking life for granted!**

Tips for Implementing Lessons

Chapter Four

Lesson 4.1 - The Power of the Brain to Change

Main Idea: Researcher Dr. Marian Diamond discovered that an enriched environment could improve brain size and performance. Her experiments with rats revealed the effects of environment on neurons and intelligence. Her shocking discovery …you can grow your brain!

Suggestions:

- Ask students to reconstruct Dr. Diamond's experiment with rats in a cartoon drawing.

- Discuss the impact of social isolation on the human brain.

- Brainstorm the following question: What does an enriched classroom environment at school look like?

Lesson 4.2 - Dr. Paul Bach-y-Rita

Main Idea: Neuroplasticity is not a myth but a powerful reality. The amazing story of Pedro Bach-y-Rita's recovery from a major stoke reaffirms the plasticity of the human brain. This inspirational story provides evidence that with continued effort, a break-through takes place, that **progress follows effort**. The adult brain has the ability to rewire and reshape itself, even after serious injury.

Suggestions:

- After reading the lesson with students, ask students to research "constraint induced therapy." Information about constraint induced therapy can be found at: http://www.circ.uab.edu/cit.htm

- Many students will have stories about family members who have experienced a stroke. Permit time for students to share their stories.

Lesson 4.3 - Living with Half a Brain

Main Idea: The story of a young girl's recovery following a radical hemispherectomy reinforced the concept that it is not the number of neurons that make the human brain work so brilliantly, but rather the number of connections between neurons that allows the brain to perform its amazing feats. Cameron's recovery demonstrates the brain's ability to rezone regions that perform one task, to assume a new role. Her case debunks the "one location, one function" myth that was once believed about the human brain.

Suggestions:

- Give students an opportunity to research the stories of other children who have undergone a hemispherectomy.

- Encourage students to read Dr. Ben Carson's new book, *Gifted Hands: The Ben Carson Story*. This book is a short, easy-to-read autobiography about one of today's leading neurosurgeons. While pursuing his career, Carson encountered and overcame prejudice, poverty, negative peer pressure, and politics to succeed. His sense of humor, faith, strong work ethic and growth mindset are highlighted in his book. In the last chapter, Carson provides recommendations to students on ways to live and to achieve.

Lesson 4.4 - My Stroke of Insight

Main Idea: The story of Dr. Jill Bolte Taylor's stroke and eight- year recovery provides further evidence of the brain's ability to repair, replace and retrain neural circuitry. With great effort and help, she challenged herself to explore, expand and develop her right hemisphere and retrain and rewire her damaged left hemisphere.

Suggestions:

- Purchase Jill Bolt's Taylor's new book, *My Stroke of Insight*, and read excerpts to your students. It is informative and inspirational.

- Assign students the task of researching the different functions of the right and left cerebral hemispheres.

- Have students explore different methods to determine if they are right-brain or left-brain dominant.

Lesson 4.5 - Dr. Merzenich's Monkey Business

Main Idea: When you focus your attention on something, the brain responds and begins to alter its physical structure. Attention and repetitive practice are needed to generate **significant** changes in the structure of the brain.

Suggestions:

- Students can have fun demonstrating the steps of the experiment through role-play.

- Dr. Merzenich has conducted many experiments as he explores the limits of neuroplasticity. Students can learn more about his research and his work on the internet.

Lesson 4.6 - Tips to Help Students Focus and Pay Attention

Main Idea: Students can strengthen their ability to focus and pay attention. Remind them, that for the brain to acquire new knowledge, it must first concentrate and pay attention.

Suggestions:

- Review the "Five Tips for Improving Focus."

- Divide students into groups of five, and have each group illustrate one of the tips on chart paper.

- Have students respond to the following writing prompt: *Tell a story about a situation when **procrastination** got you into trouble, and explain what you learned from the experience.*

Chapter Five

"If a neuron is stimulated to fire frequently, its synapse may grow stronger. Silent synapses may even begin to fire if the neuron is active enough. And, most dramatically, totally new dendrite branches and synapses may come into existence."

- James Zull

Practice Makes Permanent

It is incredible; a student can spend twelve years in school using their brain to learn, and yet, learn little if anything about the *way* their brain learns! Parents and teachers spend countless hours encouraging, begging and bribing students to practice new skills, when neither fully understands the physical effects of rehearsal and practice on brain structure. If we expect students to practice new skills and rehearse new information with the consistency and effort required to move them into long-term memory, we must help them understand that – **practice is about setting up and strengthening neural networks in the brain.** We can encourage students by sharing research that confirms; students who practice, score 21 to 44% higher on standardized tests than students who did not practice (Ross, 1988; Bloom, 1976; Kumar, 1991). When students realize the significant gains that can come with practice, they complain less about homework, and they will practice with more purpose and enthusiasm. Practice, may not make perfect, but it does, without question, make the things we do and learn more permanent.

Using simple, yet meaningful analogies, you can help students comprehend the necessity for and the power of practice. One analogy you might use; **mind-maps are like city-maps, they are constantly changing**.

Here is an activity for you to consider. I give my students two different maps of San Antonio. The first map is from 1980 (amazing what you can find digging through the glove compartment of your ten-year old car). The second map is a 2009 map of the city. Gathered around the maps, students compare them and immediately start to note their similarities and differences. New highways, subdivisions and parks appear on the new map but not the old. The city has greatly expanded northward, and the network of roads and highways has become far more complex. Old roads have given way to new wider boulevards, where the speed limits have increased from 30 mph to 55 mph.

Students typically enjoy looking at a map of their city. They are anxious to find their neighborhood, their school, their friend's street. Divide the students into two groups, one group with the old map the other group with the new map. Ask them to map out a route from their school to a distant location in the city (maybe the city zoo or a local museum). Let them discover how the new roads and highways make getting to the location easier and faster. Ask them to hypothesize what would happen if the major highways were eliminated from their route. Could they still reach their destination? Would it take longer and be more difficult?

With the maps folded and put away, try asking, "So, what did you learn from studying the two maps today?" It won't be long before someone proclaims, "Wow, the city has really grown. The network of roads and highways has really expanded." Point out that it took many years of **hard work** and **careful planning** to build those new roads, that they were an investment for the future. Imagine trying to maneuver through the city without them. Can you imagine being the mapmaker that has to keep up with all those changes?

Finally, deliver this news flash ... Just as suburban development and urban renewal change a city's map, learning and practice changes and expands your mind-maps (cortical maps). However, repeated neglect of a skill, failure to practice, lets the pathways in the brain become weak and overgrown and can eventually lead to their replacement or disappearance. Practice, practice, practice...because practice makes permanent!

The student lessons that follow chapter five will further reinforce the effects and merits of meaningful practice. Be sure to take time to discuss the reflection question found at the end of each lesson. Reflection creates connections and expands the cortical maps of the mind!

Lesson 5.1

Changing Maps of the Mind

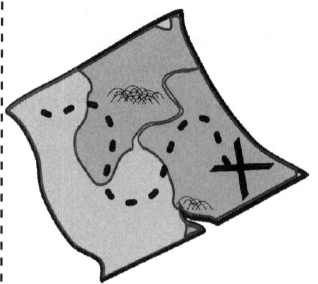

Do you remember the first maps you drew? As a young child, you may have drawn a map to your secret hiding place, to a buried treasure, or to a neighbor's house. Those early maps had only a few lines for pathways.

Later, in school, you drew maps that are more complex. These maps labeled states, countries, continents, rivers and mountain ranges. If your family went on a vacation, you may have followed a highway map. That map would have been complex, showing interstate highways, expressways, and entire networks of roads. Chances are that if your family took the same vacation a couple of years later, they probably had to buy a new map.

Maps nearly always become outdated. For example, an early map of Texas would have shown only a few roads, traveled by mule-drawn wagons, stagecoaches, or horses. One of these roads still exists, under a different name – the Old Spanish Trail. But many of those early roads simply vanished into the landscape, overgrown by weeds and thickets, or were put to some other use.

In San Antonio, Lafayette and Santa Clara Streets once ran where the Institute of Texan Cultures now stands. An entire neighborhood of very old streets was suddenly replaced by the Hemisfair area. Urban renewal, expressway construction, and other factors have phased out many city streets.

On the other hand, many new streets appear when the need or demand arises. Real estate developers create new streets around the periphery of the city in preparation for suburban housing, and those new street names appear on the latest maps. As you can guess, all of this activity creates a lot of work for mapmakers.

If you understand these ideas about streets, roads, neighborhoods, and maps, then you can understand a lot about your brain and its amazing mapmaker – the cerebral cortex.

When you were an infant, this busy mapmaker was creating new neural pathways in response to your attempts to hold up your head, scoot in your crib, and roll over. Imagine the astonishing feat of ultimately being able to feed yourself with a spoon! For a while, baby cereal escaped to the floor, got in your nose, and even in your hair. Finding your mouth was no easy feat!

The good news is that once you learned to feed yourself, you did not need to relearn the skill every time you wanted to eat. You have been practicing feeding yourself at least three times a day since you first learned with the baby cereal. Those neural pathways have become as enduring as the Old Spanish Trail or the Roman roads of Italy. Neuroscientist say, "When neurons fire together, they wire together and they get faster and function with less effort." Remember, practice makes permanent!

The bad news is that neural pathways can shrink or disappear, like overgrown roads to ghost towns. Without practice, a champion athlete becomes awkward, and too slow to compete. A leg or arm becomes stiff and useless if it is in a cast because of a broken bone. After the bone heals, special exercises or physical therapy must restore the neural pathways before normal function is possible.

There are many examples to illustrate the diminishing of cortical maps. Have you noticed how difficult it is to write your assignments in cursive after a summer without putting pen to paper? It may take you weeks to redevelop the skill.

Just as suburban development and urban renewal change a city's map, learning behavior (practice) changes your cortical maps. However, repeated neglect of a skill or failure to practice, lets the neural pathways become weak, and may eventually lead to their replacement for other purposes.

Musical Maps – Progress Follows Effort

Do you play a musical instrument? If so, you constantly create and strengthen neural pathways and cortical maps. If your instrument is a guitar or other stringed instrument, you must learn to place your fingers properly on the strings, and move them to the various places to get the right sounds. If you play the piano, unless you started as a little child, you may find that when you press one finger on a key, the other fingers pop up, (a problem that disappears with practice).

If you play the trombone, you worry about slide positions, and with that instrument and other brass and woodwind instruments, you must practice finger technique, lip control, and breathing. While faced with these challenges, you must train your eyes to follow the sheet music without constantly losing your place. Then, there is the matter of training your ears! How does anyone ever learn to make music!

The answer to that question: the brain's cortex perceives that you are trying to move your fingers a certain way, focus your eyes on a page, respond to certain sounds, etc. The brain does not immediately lay down pathways, though; the cortex requires that you make a proven commitment by repeating the actions over and over.

However, in an amazingly short time, you go from knowing almost nothing, to playing tunes that people recognize. The more you practice, the more "roads" are built and the faster you can navigate those roads.

If you look at your hands, you really can't see a difference. There may be calluses on the fingers if you play the guitar, but otherwise, there has been no transformation. If you could see inside your brain, though, you would see an expanding cortical map. The region of the motor cortex that regulates your finger, hand, and arm movements has expanded by taking over neighboring neural populations. The brain has undergone a physical change, "rounding up" neuron populations and building new pathways.

But remember, if the guitar stays on the couch or in a closet; if the piano keys get dusty; if the band instrument remains in the band hall over summer; then, you will be miserably frustrated trying to play music. The same is true of other kinds of learning as well, such as practice in math, or the memorization of certain facts.

If a person is willing to invest effort and time, the payoff is rewarding. Blind people learn to read Braille with effort, just as deaf people learn sign language. People once paralyzed because of injury or stroke can relearn how to walk.

It is really quite amazing, isn't it? Playing a musical instrument or a game of chess, learning a new language, practicing all those crazy offensive plays with your basketball teammates, all of these activities generate new cortical maps in your brain. Isn't it nice to know, that growing your brain can actually be fun!

Student Reflection Questions:

1. How does the brain respond to learning to play a musical instrument?

2. Why does a musician get "rusty" if they do not practice?

Lesson 5.2

The Brain is Plastic

The brain is plastic (changeable). It can and does remodel itself, sometimes within a remarkably short period of time.

J.M.B.

Not so long ago, scientists believed that neural pathways were laid down the first few weeks of life, and that they were unchangeable. However, because of new scientific research, we now know that these neural maps change, just as the maps of cities do.

Scientists have studied rats and monkeys to learn about brain plasticity. Rats rely heavily on their sensitive whiskers to send messages to the brain. These whiskers – like insect antennae – can tell the difference between a rigid, metal can and a chewable cardboard box (which may contain food). The cortical maps of the whiskers can change in a matter of hours, making the rat's search of a food warehouse remarkably quick and easy.

Do you remember Dr. Merzenich's experiments with the monkeys? Likewise, a monkey's cortical maps can change in a matter of days, as they practice new tasks. With repeated practice, monkeys learn to pick up a tiny piece of food, tell the difference between the voice of a predator and a friend, and track movements with their eyes that are almost unnoticeable. These changes in their brains are not a function of inherited traits. Instead, they are a function of experience.

The human brain also changes in response to experience, (just as the brains of rats and monkeys change). The activities we participate in, the friends we hang out with, the way we spend our free time and the daily choices we make, all impact and shape our brain.

Older Adults Can Learn Too

Sometimes older adults are discouraged by the stale adage, "You can't teach an old dog new tricks." Because of this negative idea, adults may be afraid to attempt to learn new skills – dancing, working on a computer, learning a new language, etc. Some see the learning process as confined by time. (I should have learned that as a kid.) Others think of it as a matter of heredity. (No one in my family can sing, so I don't even try.) Such adults need an updated lesson in neurology. Consider sharing this important message with a parent or grandparent-

The brain changes itself in response to new sensory input at any age. The key to learning is intensive, repetitive practice.

The brain has a built-in safety feature: The brain protects itself, and you, its master, by insisting on repeated demands – practice. If your cortical map of hearing changed every time you heard a new voice, you might not recognize the voice of your best friend next time he or she called! If the cortical map of your hands changed each time you tied your shoes, your hands might be too specialized to play a video game!

Remember, what differentiates the beginner in any field from the expert? Practice, practice, practice.

Carpe Diem!

This Latin expression means, "Seize the day" – take advantage of every opportunity you have. Now that you know how important instruction, study, and practice are, especially at this time in your life, decide to be in charge of your learning. The reward is beyond expectation!

Yes, a genius has to study and practice too! Actually, a genius may work much harder than the average person, because the genius has a compulsion to create, invent, compose, perform, and work! It has been said that the difference between a talented person and a genius is that the genius is absolutely compelled to develop his or her talent. Many inventors, scientists, writers, and artists have worked long hours under difficult conditions, because their genius has driven them to do so.

Genius or Hard Work

A well-known music critic visited the famous Spanish violinist and composer Pablo de Sarasate (1844-1908). The critic, amazed at his idol's skill said, "You are a genius!"

Later, Sarasate told friends, "For 37 years I have practiced fourteen hours a day, and now they call me a genius."

Student Reflection Questions:

1. Why do neuroscientists describe the human brain as plastic?

2. What is required for the brain to rewire or change its neural networks?

Lesson 5.3

Use It or Lose It - Poster Contest

Saving Neurons and Growing Dendrites

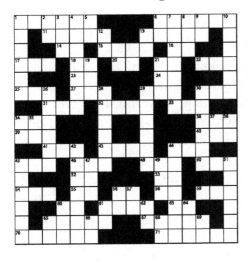

What can we do to help save neurons and grow new neural connections? Read the list of suggestions below.

1. Develop a regular mental workout.
2. Play a variety of games and participate in activities that that will challenge you mentally.
3. Read, play chess, do sudoku, complete puzzles, learn to play a musical instrument, take a photography class!
4. Make sure you have a healthy diet.
5. Get plenty of physical exercise.
6. Get enough sleep.
7. Reduce your stress.

Design a poster to illustrate the information above. Make your poster creative, colorful and informative! You might consider donating your poster to a local retirement community or nursing home!

Tips for Implementing Lessons

Chapter Five

Lesson 5.1 - Changing Maps of the Mind

Main Idea: The cortical maps of the brain, like the maps of a city, are continually undergoing change. As the neural pathways (roads) of the brain become more elaborate and better connected, the brain becomes more powerful. However, just as a road that is not traveled will become overgrown and disappear, the unused pathways of the brain diminish and may ultimately vanish.

Suggestions:

- Give students an opportunity to compare and contrast an older and newer city map.

- Ask students who play a musical instrument to describe their experience learning to play.

- Discuss the reflection questions at the end of the lesson.

Lesson 5.2 - The Brain is Plastic

Main Idea: The brain changes itself in response to new sensory information at any age. Our experiences, our friends and the daily choices we make – all of these impacts and shape the brain.

Suggestions:

- Have students research the life-story of a child prodigy. They are often surprised to learn that it takes long hours, and many years of dedicated practice, for these individuals to achieve success.

Lesson 5.3 - Use It or Lose It: Poster Contest

Main Idea: You can be proactive about saving neurons and growing new dendrites.

Suggestions:

- This is a great opportunity to let your students get creative. Their posters should be colorful and informative. They might want to consider bringing materials from home to create a collage. Ask for student volunteers to deliver the posters to area nursing homes or retirement communities.

Step 4

Life's experiences shape the brain. We have a brain that can change itself.

Evaluate current research on the effects of television, sleep deprivation, fear, and stress on the brain's structure and ability to function.

Chapter Six

The Brain That Can Change Itself

"Television's perfect. You turn a few knobs, a few of those mechanical adjustments at which the higher apes are so proficient, and lean back and drain your mind of all thought. And there you are watching the bubbles in the primeval ooze. You don't have to concentrate. You don't have to react. You don't have to remember. You don't miss your brain because you don't need it. Your heart, liver, and lungs continue to function normally. Apart from that, all is peace and quiet. You are in man's nirvana. And if some poor, nasty-minded person comes along and says you look like a fly on a can of garbage, pay him no mind. He probably hasn't got the price of a television set."

- Raymond Chandler

Two factors that significantly affect student performance and success in school are not under a teacher's control. Teachers are powerless when it comes to limiting students' television viewing time or seeing to it that they get adequate sleep. Even the most talented teachers struggle in the classroom where their audience is sleep deprived and burdened with attention problems.

Neuroscience research is revealing new information about the impact of television and sleep deprivation on the brain. Studies suggest that excessive television watching and insufficient sleep might present a far more serious problem than previously thought.

Writer Raymond Chandler's quote (above) makes an important point: Television watching generally does not require concentration, reaction or recall. In fact, it requires little if any use of the brain. All that is required, he suggests, is to lean back and drain your brain of all thought! Chandler's quote describes a brain that has shifted into neutral, one that is "zoned out." Recently however, scientists have discovered that the TV watching brain is not simply "zoned out" and disengaged, but instead may be undergoing a rewiring process. The brain, it appears, is being shaped and molded by the techniques used to deliver media.

Sadly, in some households, the TV is the first thing turned on in the morning and the last thing turned off at night. For 14-16 hours a day, it fills the house with background chatter and flashing light. While some scientists continue to debate its effect on the viewer – these new studies are sounding an important alarm. The recommendation researchers are making – limit the time your teen spends watching television and playing video games to about one to two hours a day. And when they are watching, it should be quality programming.

Why, you ask, the urgent plea for moderation in television watching? A research team lead by Jeffrey G. Johnson of Columbia College of Physicians and Surgeons, found that teens glued to the TV for three or more hours a day are at higher risk for developing attention and learning problems. The scientists noted that it was TV watching that contributed to the learning problem…not the other way around!

Johnson's team collected data on 678 families. They interviewed parents and children about their television habits and school problems. They conducted the interviews on three different occasions – when the children were 14, 16 and 22 years old. When participants in the study reached age 33, they were asked to provide information about their secondary and post-secondary education. For example, had they graduated from high school or attended college?

The study reported that at age 14, thirty-three percent of the teens reported watching TV three or more hours a day. Furthermore, it concluded that watching three or more hours of TV at age 14 was associated with:

- attention difficulties

- failure to finish homework

- boredom at school

- poor grades

- negative attitude about school

- failure to complete high school or attend college.

It is important to note, that the relationship between TV watching and negative academic outcomes was still present when socio-economic status and prior attention and learning problems were statistically controlled.

While the findings should be interpreted with caution, the conclusion appears to be a "no brainer" – **Those that watch large amounts of television are at a disadvantage in comparison to those who do not**. Yet many parents ignore warnings from the American Academy of Pediatrics and let their infants watch TV, DVDs and videos. By 3 months, 40% of babies are regular viewers. By the time children reach age 2, the number leaps to 90%! Despite the links between early television viewing and attention control, aggressive behavior and poor cognitive development, parents and teens are still not turning off their televisions. It is time to try a new approach.

The lessons that follow present evidence that television rewires and reshapes the brain. The lessons summarize the research, indicating that this reshaping and rewiring results in shortened attention spans and subsequent learning problems.

In addition, there are lessons that disclose what science is learning about the relationship between sleep and memory consolidation. Providing students with this valuable information will allow them to make informed decisions about how much sleep they get and how they spend their leisure time. These lessons reiterate that the human brain is plastic and malleable. If teens are going to chose to spend long hours watching television, playing video games and staying up all night...they need to understand the consequences of their actions. We should confront them with the available scientific evidence.

> *Without enough sleep, we all become tall two-year-olds.*
> *JoJo Jensen*

Lesson 6.1

Get to Bed!

Sleep and Learning – A Message for Teens

You know what it feels like – first the eyelids get heavy, and you'd swear they have hundred pound weights attached to them. Despite the struggle to keep them raised, they start their descent like a curtain on a stage. The head drops slowly downward, only to be abruptly jerked back just in time to prevent a head-on collision with the desk. The muscles in the neck feel like rubber, and breathing slows as you slide lower in the chair.

Today is test review day in history, and you are fighting to stay alert and focus on the lesson. Nevertheless, there you sit, your elbows perched on the desk, head cradled between your V-shaped hands, slowly losing the battle. The elbows slide apart and the head comes to a rest on the desktop. It is a habit you have maintained since your kindergartner days – taking an afternoon nap at school.

What are the findings about teens and their sleep habits? What are the effects of sleep deprivation (lack of adequate sleep) on learning? How much sleep are teens getting? Are their parents and teachers justified in nagging them to get more sleep?

In 2006, The National Sleep Foundation issued a report about teens and their sleep habits. Here are some of their findings:

1. Just one in five adolescents get an optimal nine hours of sleep on school nights; nearly one-half (45%) sleep less than eight hours on school nights.

2. More than half of adolescents report feeling tired or sleepy during the day.

3. At least once a week, more than one-quarter of high school students fall asleep in school, 22% fall asleep doing homework, and 14% arrive late or miss school because they oversleep.

4. A strong association was found between negative moods and more pronounced sleep-related issues.

5. Among those adolescents who admit to feeling unhappy or tense most of the time: 73% say that they do not get enough sleep at night, and 59% admit that they are sleepy during the day.

The conclusion: almost half of all teens are not getting enough sleep. These sleep-deprived students are more likely to nap during school and experience unhappy or negative moods. They are a sleepy, often grumpy group.

Caffeine and High Tech Toys Take a Toll on Teen Sleep

So, why are teens not getting the sleep they need in order to be happy and productive learners? The National Sleep Foundation study revealed some important clues. Consuming too much caffeine goes hand-in-hand with being overtired. Nearly one-third of all adolescents report drinking two or more caffeinated drinks per day, and as a result, they report getting less sleep.

In addition to consuming caffeine, most adolescents ignore the advice to wind down with relaxing activities one hour before bedtime. An estimated 76% watch television in the hour before bedtime, 44% surf the internet, and another 40% talk on the phone. Nearly all adolescents have at least one electronic device in their bedroom – a device that might be stealing valuable sleep time.

Your Brain is Busy While You Sleep

Cornell University professor of psychology James Maas states that not getting enough sleep negatively affects: performance, memory, learning, thinking, creativity, alertness, energy, productivity, safety, longevity, and quality of life (Power Sleep 1998). It has been documented that a person will die from lack of sleep sooner than from lack of food. Death will occur after about ten days without sleep, while starvation takes a few weeks. In short, getting adequate sleep is **really** important for both your mental and physical well-being.

Sleep, as you might expect, is closely linked with learning and success in school. Research has revealed the importance of REM sleep. REM (rapid eye movement) is the stage in the normal sleep cycle during which dreams occur. During REM sleep, the body undergoes marked changes, including rapid eye movement, loss of reflexes, and increased pulse rate and brain activity. Studies suggest that without REM sleep, students might lose what they have learned during the day. During REM sleep, the brain appears to be busy transforming daily experiences into long-term memory.

This type of sleep is associated with the consolidation of newly learned facts and experiences. During REM sleep, neural networks fire and transport memories to the hippocampus to be stored. What you learn during the day is stored and catalogued at night while you sleep. If you learn a new math concept at school during the day, but fail to get a good night's sleep afterwards, the concept will not be stored in long-term memory, and will fade. While you sleep, the brain is replaying, rehearsing and organizing the experiences of the previous day. Often when people have important decisions to make, they will say, "I need to sleep on it." Research suggests that "sleeping on it" might be a good idea. It explains why we wake up from a good night's sleep and feel "clear headed," better able to make good decisions and solve problems.

Let's say you stay up late on Tuesday night watching television, and get just five hours of sleep. Is that really such a big deal? Research suggests that you might actually lose two days of instruction because of that decision. Tuesday's lessons will not be properly reviewed and stored during REM sleep on Tuesday night, and will fade rather than be remembered. It is likely that you will miss much of Wednesday's instruction because you are sleepy and napping in classes. You will have sacrificed two of the five days of instruction for one late night of television watching. It is possible that you will learn 40% less that week than the well-rested student sitting next to you. Are your eyelids getting heavy? Did you get 8.5-9.25 hours of sleep last night?

Good Nights and Better Mornings

To help get a good night's sleep and have a happier morning, the National Sleep Foundation recommends the following:

1. Establish a relaxing bedtime routine. Try reading, taking a bath, or listening to calming music.

2. Set up a consistent bedtime and wake up time. Strive for 8.5 to 9.25 hours of sleep each night. Try to be consistent, even over the weekend.

3. Try to create a cool, dark, quiet environment in your bedroom before bedtime.

4. Keep televisions, computers and cell phones *out of the bedroom*. They will rob you of the relaxation and downtime needed to recover after a busy day at school.

5. Avoid caffeine after lunch.

6. Open window coverings and allow natural light into your bedroom in the morning.

In conclusion, studies show that the practice of specific skills followed by sleep enhances memory. After one night's sleep, even after a nap, people perform better on some memory tests related to math puzzles, to typing, and to recognizing visual patterns. Research suggests that REM sleep is important in organizing and storing experiences, and thereby enhances learning. Finally, students who are sleep deprived are more likely to experience negative moods and be unhappy.

So, shut down the computer, turn off the television, get off the phone, and get to bed! You need 8.5-9.25 hours of sleep each night. The reward for getting enough sleep... A happier, more successful you!

SLEEP LOG
Week 1: Date _____

Day of Week	Time I wake up A.M.	Time I go to sleep P.M.	Total # hours of sleep per day
Monday			
Tuesday			
Wednesday			
Thursday			
Friday			
Saturday			
Sunday			

- add up the seven numbers in the last column and divide by seven

Average number hours of sleep per day for week 1 = _____

Week 2: Date _____

Day of Week	Time I wake up A.M.	Time I go to sleep P.M.	Total # hours of sleep per day
Monday			
Tuesday			
Wednesday			
Thursday			
Friday			
Saturday			
Sunday			

- add the seven numbers in the last column and divide by seven

Average number hours of sleep per day for week 2 = _____

Do the Math

Week 1 total + Week 2 total ÷ by 2

Average number hours of sleep per day over a two week period = _____

Lesson 6.2

Cartoons Might Not Be So Funny

I wish my TV had a knob so you could turn up the intelligence. The one marked "Brightness" doesn't seem to work.

Author Unknown

Neuroscientists continue to explore the many questions surrounding the topic of brain plasticity. We know that life experiences play an important role in shaping the brain. Research has confirmed that an enriched environment can stimulate brain growth and impact intelligence. In recent years, scientists have started to ask questions about the effects of television and video games on the brain. Is the brain being rewired and shaped by these media experiences? Let's look at one recent study.

A group of scientists in the Department of Pediatrics at the University of Washington conducted a study titled: *Early Television Exposure and Subsequent Attention Problems in Children* (2004). In this study of more than 2,600 toddlers, scientists concluded that early exposure to television was associated with attention problems at age seven. The study showed that television exposure between the ages of one and three correlated with attention problems and impulse control issues later in childhood. For every hour of TV that the toddlers watched each day, their chances of developing serious attention problems at age seven increased by 10%.

While much research remains to be done on this topic, current evidence suggests that limiting television watching, particularly during the first three years of life, is highly recommended. A recent survey revealed that 43% of U.S. children two years or younger watch television daily, and that 25% have televisions in their bedrooms. As teachers of young children notice an increase in children's inability to pay attention, parents and educators have to ask the question: Can television be partly to blame?

Are You Paying Attention…

Someone next to you slams his or her locker shut with enough force to amputate a finger. The person in the bathroom stall next to you lets out a loud scream. Out of the corner of your eye, you see a grape flying across the cafeteria. Whenever you sense a quick or sudden change in the world around you, especially a sudden movement or unusual sound, you instinctively stop whatever you are doing to turn and pay attention. This "**orientation response**" evolved long ago as a protection against sudden dangerous situations. Refocusing attention on a novel or unexpected event is something humans do automatically.

Scientists are studying the "orientation response" as it relates to television and video games. They have discovered that television, music videos and video games trigger this response at a far more rapid rate than in real life. The media use edited zooms and sudden noises to **constantly redirect attention** and keep viewers and listeners focused on the television or video games. Television viewers experience a continuous "orienting response" that can leave them feeling drained after hours of viewing.

The more serious problem is that research suggests the brain is shaped and wired by the television watching process. The brain prefers this fast-paced action, and begins to require it for the viewer to keep his or her attention focused. Activities like reading, writing and listening to lectures become more difficult. The brain, hooked on the fast action of television, loses its ability to stay focused on other types of tasks. The brain experiences "boredom" when it is not being continuously redirected.

Teachers all over the country have witnessed a decrease in the "attention span" of students. A 45-minute National Geographic video that was engaging for students ten years ago cannot hold their attention for ten minutes. Teachers find that they need to "switch gears" about every 15 minutes in order to maintain students' attention. What happens to these students when they arrive at college, where the professor delivers three 60-minute lectures per week and gives two major exams for the semester? How do students who have spent thousands of hours being conditioned by the "orientation response" cope with long-term projects that require sustained effort and focus? Some estimates indicate nearly half of all freshmen who enroll in college fail to graduate. Today more than ever, students struggle with organizational skills, time management, and poor study habits. Many college students find themselves wishing they could reclaim all the hours they spent in high school watching television and playing video games. They wish that they could rewire and reprogram their brains.

Next time you watch a television commercial, examine the techniques used to refocus and redirect your attention. Can you detect when you are experiencing an "orientation response"? Are you having a brain altering experience?

Lesson 6.3

Listen to the Beat

Stop Stepping on My Feet!

There you stand, tucked into a far corner of the school gym, huddled with a few friends who probably feel as awkward as you do. You watch everyone else having fun, marveling as they do one of those line dances – long strands of kids, moving as a single unit, twisting, turning and keeping a perfect beat. How did they learn to dance? Did they come from a long line of professional dancers, or is there a secret to learning those smooth moves?

If you ask a few people how they learned to dance, they will probably say that the first steps they learned were taught **verbally** and **visually**. In other words, someone **talked** them through the steps, and **showed** them the moves at the same time. The lesson might have sounded something like, "one – two, cha-cha-cha, 3 – 4 cha, cha, cha." Or if they were learning to do the Texas two-step, it might have been, "slow-slow-quick-quick, slow-slow-quick-quick." The first dance lesson includes *hearing* the instruction and *visualizing* the dance movements.

Next comes the hard part. After listening to the instruction, and watching several demonstrations, you need to translate that auditory and visual information into motion. That's right, you have to leave the security of the gym corner and start moving! When you are first learning, you will find that dancing requires thinking (left side of the brain), serious concentration (frontal lobe), and self-direction (speech). You will likely have to count aloud and visualize the moves in your head as you perform them. The slightest distraction will throw you off and result in a misstep. It is safe to say, that at this stage it is best to practice without an audience!

After days or weeks of practice, something amazing happens. The sequence of steps and the movements become a **motor routine**. Suddenly, you realize that the body will execute the sequence automatically, upon the brain's command. You stop counting, stop visualizing, and start dancing. The brain is on autopilot!

A **motor routine** is established when verbal and visual information becomes encoded in the **cerebellum** (the ball-shaped structure located at the base of the brain). The cerebellum coordinates movements, making them smoother and more fluid. Then, unlike when you were first learning, you are finally free to dance, talk, and chew gum – all at the same time!

In recent years, neuroscientists have discovered evidence that the cerebellum is involved in coordinating **thought patterns** as well as movement patterns. Dr. Jay Giedd, a neuroscientist from the National Institute of Mental Health, discovered that the cerebellum plays a crucial role in coordinating thought processes and making decisions. A strong, well-exercised cerebellum is essential for efficient problem-solving skills. Regular exercise, such as dancing, strengthens the neurons in the cerebellum, preventing them from being pruned or eliminated. A strong and healthy cerebellum will permit you to solve that difficult, multi-step math problem or to write the lengthy, reflective essay.

Remember, for the brain to acquire new information, you must first **listen** to and **visualize** the information. Next, you must repeat and rehearse the information. Finally, you need to put the new information into motion … that is, do something with it. You might draw a picture, solve a math problem, conduct an experiment, or create a graphic organizer. As you rehearse and repeatedly use the information to solve problems, it becomes encoded in the cerebellum, giving you mental dexterity.

Summary: Four steps to achieving smooth, coordinated thoughts.

1. Listen carefully to the new information.

2. Visualize the new information in your mind, creating a mental picture.

3. Rehearse (repeat) the information several times.

4. Put the information into motion, do something with it!

Tips for Implementing Lessons

Chapter Six:

Lesson 6.1 – Get to Bed

Main Idea: Most teens and preteens do not get enough sleep. Insufficient sleep negatively affects learning and memory. This lesson provides data on teens' sleep habits, and offers sound tips to help students get a good night's sleep.

Suggestions:

- Have students keep a sleep log for a two- week period.

- Survey students to find out how many have televisions and/or computers in the bedroom. Suggest that they experiment by removing them (television and/or computer) from the bedroom for a month – to see if the change has a positive effect on their school performance. If students cannot commit to a month, suggest they try the experiment for a week!

Lesson 6.2 – Cartoons Might Not be So Funny

Main Idea: Research suggests that watching television and playing video games can alter brain structure. Recent studies have documented that early exposure to television is associated with increased attention problems in some children.

Suggestions:

- Allow your students to watch a 10-15 minute cartoon program. Have them document the techniques used in the program to generate the "orientation response."

- Discuss the television watching habits of teens. Have students calculate the average number of hours they spend watching television each day.

Lesson 6.3 – Listen to the Beat

Main Idea: Learning to dance requires listening, visualizing, rehearsing, and moving. You can use the same procedures when acquiring any new skill, or when learning any new information. The process is all about establishing a motor routine, and training the cerebellum.

Suggestions:

- Get student volunteers to teach the class a line dance (electric slide is a favorite). Allow the students to practice the dance regularly for a few minutes each day until they can perform it without thinking about the movements.

Chapter Seven

"Never let the fear of striking out get in your way."

- George Herman "Babe" Ruth

Fear & Learning

Students with a fixed mindset are often fraught with fear. When faced with a challenge, they fear embarrassment and failure. The fear they experience is real, and powerful enough to block learning and impede success in school. However, when students understand *how* fear obstructs the problem-solving process, they are more willing to face these fears and deal with them. Students must understand that fear compromises cognitive abilities. **Low** threat and **high** challenge is good, **high** threat and **high** challenge results in a disastrous learning environment.

You might consider starting the school year with a biology lesson about fear and learning (see student lesson 7.1). Remind students that we are all fearful under certain situations, but that it is important not to allow fear to disrupt learning.

Read the student lesson "Fear Can Block Learning", and open the floor to discussion. Together with your students, compile a list of fears and stressors that they might experience at school. You might be amazed at how long the list can get!

If students are reluctant to talk about the things they fear most at school, or if they need help getting started, try providing them with a list. Ask them to write about which "fear" on the list they most identify with and tell why. This could be the most important writing prompt students respond to all year. It can provide you with valuable information that helps develop individual student profiles. These can then guide you in formulating your classroom procedures.

A list of "fears" commonly expressed by students:

- I might fail, even if I try
- I will look stupid if I ask a question
- I am not "smart" enough
- I will be bullied or made fun of because I don't "fit in"
- I will lose my friends or not have friends
- I might have a teacher that does not like me
- I will disappoint my parents
- I will never be able to afford to go to college
- I will be asked to read aloud in class
- I will never understand math
- I just do not have what it takes to be successful in school

Note that several items on the list reflect students with a **fixed mindset**. This is a great opportunity to introduce the concept of the *two mindsets,* and to begin sharing stories about the amazing **plasticity** of the human brain.

Yes, we are each born with a unique brain structure, and we all have strengths and weaknesses in our neural networks. However, each of us has the potential to sculpt and construct a better brain through effort and practice. At this point, let your students know, that as a teacher, you are there to help them develop their strengths and minimize their weaknesses.

You might also consider discussing the following list of possible student stressors compiled by Martha Kaufeldt (1999). Then, reflect on your classroom environment, teaching style, and methods. Look for opportunities to reduce fear and stress in your classroom.

Martha Kaufeldt's list of possible student stressors:

- emotional threats, embarrassment, put-downs
- demonstrated disrespect for self, culture, or social group
- inadequate time to complete a task
- lack of time for reflection and expansion
- predetermined correct outcomes established by an external agent
- unfamiliar work with little support for learning
- lack of orderliness and coherence
- physical and social isolation
- unknown purpose, schedule, or agenda
- lack of information about task, behavior expectations, or goals
- punishments for failure, such as loss of privileges
- competition and extrinsic rewards
- perceived irrelevance and lack of personal meaning

After students learn about the biological response to fear, help them brainstorm about strategies for calming the fears that they may be experiencing in school. Ask questions like, "What should you do if you are afraid to read aloud in class? What strategies might we use to help someone overcome the fear of reading aloud?"

When students brainstorm about strategies, and begin to realize that many students experience fear, their own anxieties begin to subside. Imagine the relief when a student learns that others in their class are likewise fearful of public speaking and reading aloud. One student proclaimed during this discussion, "I heard that people fear public speaking more than death, and I think I'm one of them!"

It is important for students to know that their teachers are empathic and committed to helping them be successful. Try sharing a personal story about fear with your students. A well-crafted personal narrative can be powerful – opening a line of communication between student and teacher that otherwise might never develop.

Remember, when students are fearful, they often experience emotional outbursts. When that occurs, use the opportunity to talk with them about quieting their "emotional brain" so they can better develop and utilize their "thinking brain". As they begin to understand that fear and stress have a negative impact on their futures; they slowly begin to reel in their emotions and become more rational problem solvers – and that is a beautiful event to behold!

Lesson 7.1
Fear Can Block Learning

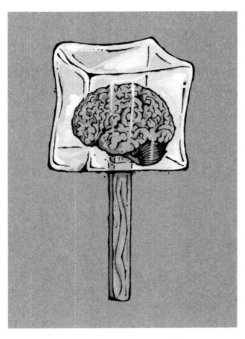

Anna hated her history class. The teacher frequently called on students to stand and read aloud from the textbook. There was no discernable pattern to the selection process. Occasionally Anna would sit through the entire class period, waiting to be called upon, and quietly praying that she would not be selected.

Anna was a good student and a competent reader, but she was terrified of reading aloud in front of her peers. The very thought of it made her stomach knot up, her muscles tense, and her heart race. On one occasion, she stumbled over several new words, mispronouncing them, and the entire class cracked-up laughing. Despite the teacher's disapproval, some kids continued to snicker whenever a student mispronounced a word.
Anna's history grades plummeted.

"It's like my brain is in freeze mode," Anna explained. "I can't hear anything except this little voice in my head repeating, 'Please don't let me be next!' I can't seem to learn or remember anything in history. I'm just a nervous wreck in that class." Fear had created a roadblock to learning, and had high-jacked the thinking (cognitive) part of Anna's brain.

Most people realize that the brain constantly talks to the body, telling it to breathe, to move, to eat, to sleep, etc. Did you know that your body also talks to your brain? Millions of cellular wires (nerves) send messages back and forth between the brain and the body. This two-way conversation is important so that the brain can sense what is happening moment by moment, within the body and around it.

In addition to the nerve signals, the brain also produces *chemicals* that are deposited directly into the bloodstream. These chemicals have a very important role; they provide the body with information about what the brain is experiencing. The brain, in turn, also picks up chemicals produced by the body; chemicals that tell the brain what the body is experiencing. The two must stay in close communication.

The chemicals produced by the brain and the body are powerful. They are responsible for feelings and desires, allowing us to feel happiness, pleasure, anger, depression and **fear**. They make us aware of what we are sensing.

Before we can understand how feelings such as fear interfere with learning, we need to identify a structure in the most "ancient" part of the human brain, the **amygdala**. The amygdala has been nicknamed the "fear center." It plays a role in other emotions, but fear and its related emotion, anger, seem to originate in the amygdala. The amygdala tells us when we are in DANGER! When the brain receives sensory information (from eyes, ears, nose, touch and taste), it sends that information directly to the amygdala. The amygdala filters all of this incoming information and, like a good guard dog, stands ready to protect us – constantly monitoring our experiences, looking for signs of danger. Our survival and safety depend on the efficiency of this monitoring system!

When the amygdala senses danger and activates, changes start to happen quickly. First, the **hypothalamus** is activated, triggering a chemical signal for danger which is received by the **adrenal glands**, a pair of glands located near the kidneys. In response, the adrenal glands release a chemical called **adrenaline** into the bloodstream. It is this chemical that increases the heart rate, elevates blood pressure, and tenses the muscles. Adrenaline generates the energy necessary to run or fight in self-defense. As adrenaline floods the body, we experience fear, which makes us very uncomfortable, and when we remain in a fearful situation, physical changes generate stress on the body.

Exactly how does fear block learning? Research shows that adrenalin **blocks** or inhibits the function of the frontal-cortex (the thinking, problem-solving part of the brain). When we are in a highly emotional state, we lose access to the CEO (problem-solving) portion of the brain. Instead, the brain gives priority to processing incoming information that poses a threat to survival. In short, it is hard to think, solve a problem or make good decisions when we are in the state of "FEAR." When the amygdala activates, the top priority becomes flight or fight, not think or create! Fear can create a real physical block to learning as your emotional brain (which includes the amygdala) ambushes your thinking brain. When you are fearful, it is very difficult to think logically, recall important information, or make good choices. It's no wonder people do such crazy things when they are afraid!

To improve learning, you must identify and reduce perceived threats in the classroom. The problem is not "all in your head" – meaning a product of imagination. Fear is in the brain, in the body, and in the many wires and chemicals that allow communication. Conquer fears, calm the amygdala, and let learning and problem solving begin!

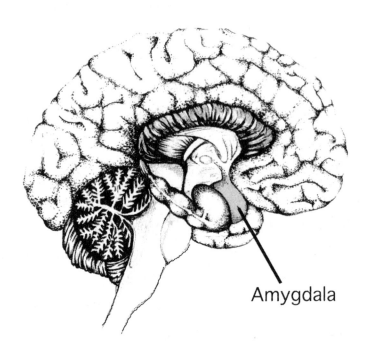

The Amygdala or "Fear Center"

Lesson 7.2

Why Middle School is Scary

Many students are scared silly when they start middle school. They are excited about having new freedoms, but fearful of the many unknowns they will face. What are students most afraid of as they move from elementary to middle school? An informal survey revealed seven common concerns and fears students experience when starting middle school. See if you can list the top seven "fears." Compare your list with a partner. When you finish, ask your teacher for the list the survey provided.

1.

2.

3.

4.

5.

6.

7.

Tips for Implementing Lessons

Chapter Seven

Lesson 7.1 – Fear Can Block Learning

Main Idea: Research shows that adrenalin (the hormone released into the body when we experience fear) inhibits the functioning of the frontal cortex, which is the problem-solving part of the brain.

Suggestions:

- Several suggestions appear in chapter seven of the teacher's text. Be sure to discuss *Martha Kaufeldt's* list of possible student stressors.

Lesson 7.2 – Why Middle School is Scary

Main Idea: Transitioning from elementary to middle school is often difficult for students. Many middle school students share the same concerns and worries.

Suggestions:

- Provide students with the results of the informal survey, and encourage them to discuss different ways to deal with these concerns:

  1. Locker combinations
  2. Being late for class
  3. Not having friends
  4. Facing the cafeteria
  5. Classes being too difficult
  6. Getting lost
  7. Being too different

- Have students write a short essay about a fearful situation they encountered at school, and describe how they dealt with it.

Step 5

Memory is a skill. As a result, you can train and improve your memory. Students of all ages can benefit greatly from sharpening their memory skills, and using specific strategies and techniques to enhance learning and recall.

Teach "brain friendly" strategies that boost student confidence while enhancing learning and improving memory.

Chapter Eight

The true art of memory is the art of attention.

- Samuel Johnson

Brain-Friendly Strategies

To Improve Memory

What is memory?

Simply put, memory is the mental challenge of recalling information that you have learned or experienced. A good memory can result in achievement and success at school, while a fuzzy memory can result in poor grades and frustration. Reviewing the "seven tips to improving memory" with students will bolster their self-confidence and significantly improve their ability to both retain and retrieve information. Do not assume that your students are familiar with these strategies. Even if they are, reviewing them again can be helpful. See tip seven about over-learning!

Seven Tips to Improve Memory & Recall

1. **Focus your attention.** Do not attempt to multitask: It takes about eight seconds of intense focus to process a single piece of information through the hippocampus (a primitive structure deep in the brain that plays the single largest role in processing information as memory). Multitasking might seem like a good idea but it is actually a distraction for the brain. Researchers from the University of California at Los Angeles found that people who learn something new while multitasking are less likely to be able to recall the new information later. Neuroscientists speculate that distractions that are present when you are trying to create a new memory tend to become tangled up with the new information. Later, when you are attempting to recall the information, you end up needing the distraction, to be able to get the information back out of storage. For example, if you listen to music on your ipod while studying for a test, you end up needing the music to be able to recall what you learned. In short, multitasking appears to hinder memory. (See Lesson 8.1)

2. **Know your learning style:** Most students tend to be visual learners; they learn best by reading, observing, and by creating a mental image of the information they are learning. Visual learners benefit from using picture cues, highlighting text, and making note cards. Other students are auditory learners and learn best by listening. These students should be encouraged to record information and to listen to it until they can remember it. Still, other students prefer a tactile experience and benefit from building models and conducting experiments.

3. **Use a multi-sensory approach:** Use all learning pathways in the brain (visual/auditory, kinesthetic-tactile) in order to enhance memory and learning. Relate information to color, texture, taste and smell. For example, in describing the brain, you might say: it has the texture of a ripe avacado, is wrinkled like a walnut and about the size of a cantelope. These types of comparisions generate stronger memories.

4. **Organize information:** Remember, the more you manipulate it (information) the better you remember it; encourage students to create concept maps, outlines,

timelines, note cards, graphic organizers, visual elaborations, acronyms and acrostics.

5. **Rehearse, rehearse, rehearse:** Review new material the same day that you learned it and plan to revisit it every few days until you are confident you can remember it. Typically, "spaced rehearsal" is better than cramming. New evidence suggests that reviewing information just before going to sleep will help "cement" the information more firmly in memory, so read over class notes before signing off at night.

6. **Connect** new information to prior knowledge: Remember, learning takes place when neurons connect. When processing new material, take time to reflect on like information stored in memory. Ask yourself, "How is this (new information) similar to information I have learned previously?" Connecting takes time and requires reflective thought. Learning is active not passive. You must actively search your memory, looking for similarities and connections. Reflective writing improves ones ability to read critically, analyze new ideas and connect them to past knowledge. Provide your students with guidelines (See Lesson 8.2) and encourage reflective writing.

7. **Be patient and have a positive outlook**: Telling yourself that you have a poor memory will actually hinder your ability to remember. Utilize several different memory strategies and expect to be successful. A positive mental outlook facilitates both understanding and recall. Remember, you can strengthen and improve your memory with practice.

The brain is like a muscle, the more you exercise it, the more it grows. The same holds true for memory. You can strengthen your memory by deliberately exercising it. Select favorite poems or song lyrics and attempt to memorize them. Play concentration-style memory games and card games that rely on focus and recall.

One recent study (Shea 2007) suggests that eating a couple of apples a day may strengthen memory. In a novel animal study, adult mice (9-12 months-old) and older mice (2-2.5 years old), were fed three different diets (a standard diet, a nutrient-deficient diet, and a nutrient-deficient diet supplemented with apple juice concentrate). After multiple assessments of memory and learning using traditional maze tests, researchers found that the mice who consumed the apple juice-supplemented diets performed significantly better on the maze tests. "It was astonishing how the animals on the apple-enhanced diets did a superior job on the maze tests, outperforming those mice not on the supplemented diet," remarks Dr. Shea.

Apples, it seems, have just the right dose of antioxidants to raise levels of acetylcholine, a neurotransmitter that is essential to memory. In addition, scientists believe that antioxidants found in apples help preserve memory by protecting neurons from free radicals created by everyday metabolic action. So, when students have a big test coming their way, suggest that they munch a couple of apples per day!

Lesson 8.1

Effects of Environment on Memory

Laboratory Investigation

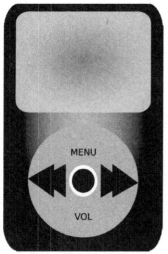

Do you listen to music while you study? If you close your eyes, does it help you to concentrate? Have you ever wondered if environmental factors can have an effect on memory? Let's investigate.

Purpose: In this laboratory investigation, you will explore the effects of a variety of environmental factors on the ability of students to recall lists of words. You will investigate the varying effects of changing conditions on memory.

Materials:

Vocabulary lists
Music CD
Blindfold (scarf)
Two plastic bags with ice

Procedure: Divide the class into research groups. Each group should consist of three students:

- One student to collect data
- One student to serve as subject
- One student to serve as researcher

Step 1:

Control Group: The control group will be tested under normal classroom conditions. The researcher will repeat a series of predetermined words beginning with three and adding one word at a time, until the subject cannot correctly repeat the list.

Repeat the test three times, using a new list of words and record the data.

Note: Groups can use any vocabulary words as long as they have similar numbers of syllables. Example: stop, wait, run, fall, hop.

Step 2:
Music: The subject will repeat the above process but with the addition of sound. Play some moderately loud music as they perform the test. (Caution: you do not want to damage hearing). Conduct three trials; and record the data. Remember, you are testing the effects of external sound on memory. All conditions remain the same, except for the addition of music.

Step 3:
Cold: Next, have the subject lay his or her, hands on the table with the palms turned upward. Place a plastic bag filled with ice on each hand. Wait three minutes before repeating the test with a new list of words. Perform three trials and record the data.

Step 4:
Darkness: Finally, place a blindfold over the subject's eyes to block out light. Conduct three trials using a new list of words and record the data.

Data Table:

Number of words recalled correctly

Trials	Control	Music	Ice	Darkness
1				
2				
3				
Average				

Analysis of data:

Study and discuss the data your research group has collected. Answer the following questions.

1. Under which conditions could the subject remember the most words?

2. Was the subject adversely (negatively) affected by any of the environmental conditions? Explain.

3. Can you draw any conclusions from the data collected about the effects of environmental conditions on learning? Explain.

Lesson 8.2

The Power of Personalized Reflection

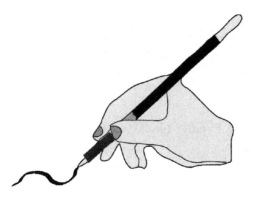

A 2007 survey conducted by the Pew American Life Project asked teens about the importance of writing skills. A surprising 86% said they believed that writing skills were important or essential for success. Most students want to learn how to compose a research report, write a resume, and express thoughts and beliefs in writing. They understand that those skills are important, yet they resist practicing how to write.

"The only way to learn to write is to write."
Peggy Teeters

Learning Begins with Reflection

Reflection is an important part of the learning process. Reflective writing improves your ability to read critically and analyze new ideas, and helps to clarify your understanding. The reflection process is a complex mental activity involving memory, analysis, and high-level thought. Reflection creates a bridge between previously acquired information and new data, so that learning can take place. There is power in the process of personal reflection.

Guidelines for Reflective Writing

When creating a written reflection, include the following features:

1. Description- Briefly **describe** your experience (class activity or reading).

2. Impact- Tell what you have learned and how you **feel** about what you have learned. React to what you have read or done by agreeing or disagreeing.

3. Intent (Action) - Write a statement about what you **intend to do** because of your learning and feelings. Be specific and give examples. Phrase your writing in a personal and positive way ("What I will do . . .." rather than "What I won't do . . .").

Reflective writing takes time and requires thought …so do not rush. Think about what you already know, what you have learned and how this will influence your actions in the future. Reflection is NOT a one-word answer.

Remember, writing skills take time and practice to develop and are important for your success. Writing and learning begin with **reflection**!

"By three methods, we may learn wisdom: First, by reflection, which is noblest; second, by imitation, which is easiest; and third by experience, which is the bitterest."

Confucius

Lesson 8.3

Mind-Sketching

Using Visual Elaboration to Learn New Vocabulary

Napoleon Bonaparte, the infamous French general, once said "Un bon croquis vaut mieux qu'un long discours," or "A good sketch is better than a long speech." Perhaps you have heard the expression, "a picture is worth a thousand words." With these two quotes in mind, let's explore **visual elaboration**, a strategy that can help you build better vocabulary skills. This technique uses mental pictures to cue vocabulary definitions. I call it mind-sketching!

This is how it works:

1. Carefully read the new vocabulary word and definition.

2. Rewrite the definition, putting it into your own words. This will help increase your ability to understand and remember the new word.

3. Develop a mental picture that represents the definition in some way.

4. Draw the picture on paper. Don't worry about the quality of the drawing; just make sure it represents the newly defined word.

5. Practice recalling the definition by looking at the picture of each word. Think of the picture as you say each word. Explain to a partner how the pictures you have drawn represent the definitions.

6. Practice until you can recall each definition by just hearing or seeing the word, without using the picture.

Now grab a copy of your new vocabulary words from English or reading class and give **visual elaboration** a try!

Lesson 8.4

Acronyms Activate Memory (AAM)

You use them every time you send a text message. But have you ever used acronyms to study for a test? Acronyms are invented combinations of letters where each letter is the initial of a word you want to remember. (Example: PTA is an acronym for Parent Teacher Association.)

Many acronyms have become so commonplace, that they are considered valid in the game SCRABBLE. You can check out the Official Scrabble Player's Dictionary, 4th Edition, to find out which acronyms are acceptable when playing the game!

How many of these acronyms can you decode? Write you answers next to the acronym. When you are finished, check out the answers on the back! LOL- Lots of Luck!

AAK	MYOB
ADN	MIA
AI	MVP
ASAP	NASA
BTW	OOT
COD	OTL
FDROFL	POW
HAND	TLC
IMHOL	UFO
LOL	VIP

Acronym Answers:

AAK (asleep at the keyboard)

ADN (any day now)

AI (as if)

ASAP (as soon as possible)

BTW (by the way)

COD (cash on deliver)

FDROFL (falling down, rolling on floor laughing)

HAND (have a nice day)

IMHO (in my humble opinion)

LOL (laughing out loud or lots of love)

MYOB (mind your own business)

MIA (missing in action)

MVP (most valuable player)

NASA (national aeronautics and space administration)

OOT (out of town)

OTL (out to lunch)

POW (prisoner of war)

TLC (tender loving care)

UFO (unidentified flying object)

VIP (very important person)

Lesson 8.5

Acrostics

Acrostics can help you recall specific information about a new topic. Suppose, you were learning about the human skeletal system and needed to be able to list characteristics of that system. You could make an acrostic to help you remember important details. Creating an acrostic requires examination and reorganization of the new information. It requires that the brain create new connections and as a result, strengthens understanding and recall.

Example

S- Supports the body

K- Keeps organs protected

E- Enables you to move

L- Long bones make up your arms and legs

E- Eating calcium-rich foods keeps bones strong

T- Tendons attach muscles to bones

O- Osteocyte is the scientific name for a bone cell

N- New blood cells are made in the marrow of certain bones

Lesson 8.6

It's All Greek to Me!

"But those that understood him smiled at one another and
shook their heads; but, for mine own part, it was Greek to me."
William Shakespeare

When people do not understand something, when something makes absolutely no sense to them, they may use the expression "it's all Greek to me." Greek, it turns out, is one of the most difficult languages to learn (which explains why few people outside of Greece can speak it). Fortunately, you will probably never have to become fluent in Greek, but there is a good chance that you will be required to learn many Greek root words.

Why Learn Greek and Latin Roots?

The English language has its roots in several languages, including Greek, Latin, older forms of English, German, and French. Learning to recognize common roots and affixes (prefixes and suffixes) will help you build your vocabulary and improve your ability to make educated guesses about unknown words you encounter in reading and test-taking situations. Learn one root and you have the key that will unlock the meanings of up to ten, twenty, or even hundreds of English words in which that Latin and/or Greek element (prefix, root, or suffix) appears.

Fun with Greek and Latin Roots

Imagine being able to determine the meanings of thousands of English words that you have never seen before! That is the power of learning Greek and Latin root words. However, memorizing long lists of roots can be difficult and, frankly, not much fun. To help yourself learn and remember Greek and Latin roots try this:

1. Combine two or three Greek or Latin roots to create a nonsense word.

2. Using the meaning of the roots as a guide, develop a definition for the nonsense word you have created. Example: logos = word; phobia = fear of: logophobia!

3. Illustrate the word with a picture

4. Write a definition for your new nonsense word.

Check out this example. Illustrate the new word Jacioskopelogist in the space provided. Remember, be creative and have fun. Share your illustration with a partner and see if they can guess which root words you used.

Jacioskopeologist

Illustrate the new word in the space below.

Jacio
Throw
(Latin)

Skopeo
Inspect, examine
(Latin)

Logos
Study
(Greek)

Jacioskopeologists - A scientist that uses a special magnifying scope to inspect and study flying objects that are now stuck to the ceilings in local middle school cafeterias.

Tips for Implementing Lessons

Chapter Eight

Lesson 8.1 - Effects of Environment on Memory

Main Ideas: Multitasking might seem like a good idea, but research shows that it is actually a distraction for the brain. In this investigation, students explore the effects of different environmental factors on memory. Their results should reveal that playing moderately loud music while learning new information has a negative effect on memory. In addition, some students may find that holding ice bags in their hands will result in improved recall. Why? The coldness produces an **increased alertness**, and as a result, the students are better able to recall the needed facts.

Suggestions:

- Science teachers on staff might be interested in doing this activity with the students. It is an excellent opportunity for students to conduct a scientific investigation. Students will collect data, graph data, and interpret results.

Lessons 8.2 – 8.4

Main Idea: Students can learn strategies, such as visual elaboration, acronyms, and acrostics to increase understanding and improve recall.

Suggestions:

- Review the "Seven Tips for Improving Memory and Recall" with students. Ask students to analyze their predominant learning style. Are they visual, auditory or tactile learners?

- Provide examples of each strategy, and guide students as they implement the different techniques in order to acquire and solidify new information.

Closing Thoughts

Teacher to Teacher

Every teacher has designed a lesson that on paper seemed to be a great idea but when field-tested in the classroom, proved to be a disaster. My most memorable catastrophe was a science lab titled "Why Snot." The lab procedures called for the students to create a mixture of corn syrup and white school glue. The thinking was that making the sticky concoction would help the kids appreciate the consistency and function of the mucus that lines the respiratory system. Not being one who gives up easily, I allowed the kids to go through 180 Dixie cups, four large bottles of corn syrup, and a gallon of glue before I finally put a stop to the lab investigation. At the end of the day, the kids were still clueless about the function of mucus in the respiratory system, and had only succeeded in coating their lab tables with a thick, sticky goo that took days to remove.

With the "Why Snot" lab in mind, I was determined to field-test every lesson suggested in this book before including it. Between 2007-2009, I conducted two separate pilot programs using the *Aim to Grow Your Brain* stories and lessons. Teachers and students participating in the pilot programs offered feedback and comments, and only those lessons that received their highest stamp of approval appear in this book.

It is difficult to describe just how **powerful** the *Aim to Grow Your Brain* stories and lessons can be for some students. After describing Marion Diamond's discovery that rats can grow their intelligence, a 7th grade girl with tear-filled eyes looked up at me and said, *"Are you saying that I can get smart if I want to? That I don't have to be dumb?"*

One young man summed up the program perfectly when he said,

> *"Why didn't someone tell us this before? I never knew that I could actually grow my brain. Now I know that if I am not so smart at something, I can fix it, and get smarter. Come on now... if rats can grow their brains, surely I can too!"*

It will be up to each individual teacher to decide how best to incorporate the ***Aim to Grow Your Brain*** lessons and stories into the classroom. In this era of high-stakes testing and accountability, teachers struggle to cover their core content, and time is a precious commodity. I recall plowing through my "scope and sequence," though, only to discover that – at the end – some students had been left behind. I had dismissed these underachievers, labeling them lazy and unmotivated. I now know that what they needed was a mindset adjustment. They needed to know and understand that:

> *"Smart is something you get, not something you are. If you embrace new challenges, give your best effort, and practice faithfully, you will grow in intelligence. We all have the potential to grow a better brain."*

Deliver this message of hope... and watch lives change.

Acknowledgments

Thank you, Marie Loomis for your friendship and editing skills, both were invaluable in the process on writing *Aim to Grow Your Brain*. Thank you to Anne, Chet, Bonnie, Marlene, Sean, Katie, Patty and Henri for your careful reading of the manuscript and thoughtful suggestions. Thank you to the teachers and students at Eisenhower Middle School in San Antonio, Texas that participated in the *Aim to Grow Your Brain* pilot programs. Finally, I want to extend a very special thank you to my husband, Lee. Thank you, Lee, for tolerating the many long hours, weeks and months I spent researching and writing and for *always* being my most ardent supporter

References

Begley, Sharon (2007). *Train Your Mind Change Your Brain*. New York: Random House

Blakeslee, Sandra and Blakeslee, Matthew (2007). *The Body Has a Mind of Its Own*. New York: Random House

Bolte Taylor, J (2006). *My Stroke of Insight*: A Brain Scientists Personal Journey. New York, NY: Penguin Books.

Carter, Rita (2000). *Mapping the Mind*. Phoenix: Orion House

Dweck, Carol S. (2006) *Mindset*. New York: Random House

Diamond, Marian and Hopson, Janet (1998). Magic *Trees of the Mind*. New York: Penguin Group.

Diamond, M.C., (1988). Enriching Heredity: The Impact of the Environment on the Anatomy of the Brain. New York: Free Press.

Doidge, Norman (2007). *The Brain That Changes Itself*. New York: Penguin Books.

Gage, F., Van Praag, H., Kempermann, G., R: Running increases cell proliferation and neurogenesis in adult mouse dentate gyrus. *Nature Neuroscience*, 2(3): 266-70.

Giedd, J., (1999). Brain development during childhood and adolescences: A longitudinal MRI study. *Nature Neuroscience*, 2(10), 861-3.

Haskel, S. (1971). *Fundamental Concepts of Modern Biology*. New York: AMSCO

Howard, Pierce J. (2006). *The Owner's Manual for the Brain* (Third Edition).Bard Press

Karten, Y.J.G., Olariv, A. & Cameron, H.A. 2005. Stress in early life inhibits neurogenesis in adulthood. *Trends in Neuroscience*, 28(4), 171-172.

Merzenich, M.M, (1998). Cortical map reorganization enabled by nucleus basalis activity. Science, 279 (5357): 1714-18.

Nicholls, J.G (1990). What is ability and why are we mindful of it? A developmental perspective. Competence Considered (pp.11-40) New Haven, CT; Yale University Press

Pink, Daniel H. (2006). *A Whole New Mind*. New York: Penguin Group.

Snyder, C.R., (1994). *The Psychology of Hope*. Kansas: Free Press.

Sur, M., Von Melchner, I., Pallas, I., "Visual Behavior Mediated by Retinal Projections Directed to the Auditory Pathways," Nature 404 (2000): 871-75.

Zull, James (2002) *The Art of Changing the Brain*. Sterling, VA: Stylus Publishing, LLC.

About the Author

Joanne Billingsley is an educational consultant, keynote speaker and lecturer. She has over twenty years of classroom experience, teaching elementary, middle and high school students. She currently works as a science & learning-center specialist and conducts professional development seminars. Joanne is a faculty member at Texas A&M University-San Antonio and an adjunct lecturer with the Texas Educational Service Center Region 20. She is the recipient of numerous teaching awards, including **Texas Teacher of the Year 2007 (ECS 20)** and the KENS-5 Excellence in Teaching Award. An active member of the Learning and Brain Society and the Mind Science Foundation, she has the expertise to assist schools in interpreting and applying current neuroscience and scientifically based educational research. Most importantly, Joanne possesses a passion for working with and inspiring teachers and students.

Joanne resides in San Antonio, Texas with her husband Lee. Together they raised three wonderful children, Anne, Michael and Matthew and now share the joy of spending time with their two granddaughters Julia Mae Williams and Eleanor Agnes Billingsley.

You can contact her via E-mail at: jbillingsley@satx.rr.com. or visit her Web site – www.jmbillingsley.com

CPSIA information can be obtained
at www.ICGtesting.com
Printed in the USA
FSOW03n0111180717
36183FS